FIGHT & WIN

Brock Evans's Strategies
for the New Eco-Warrior

Brock Evans

Barclay
Bryan Press

Barclay Bryan Press, Inc.

FIGHT & WIN: Brock Evans's Strategies for the New
    Eco-Warrior

First North American edition

Photographs courtesy of James Dougherty and Brock Evans.
Stock images reproduced with permission from Fotolia™,
Shutterstock™, and iStock™.

Book design by Words & Pictures, Inc.
Book jacket image by James Brown
Book jacket design by William Bryan

Library of Congress Cataloging in Publication registration
pending

ISBN 978-0-578-13295-2

Advance Praise for **FIGHT & WIN**

This gem of a book by the legendary environmentalist Brock Evans should be read by everyone who cares about the future of our planet. Full of inspirational stories, practical advice, and pithy wisdom, readers of Fight & Win *will learn how to fight entrenched commercial and industrial interests who are more focused on short-term profits than the health and well-being of future generations. A must-read for aspiring eco-warriors and citizen activists.*

Award-winning environmental filmmaker/author Chris Palmer

I've known Brock Evans as a leader among conservation activists through two generations. Now, in Fight & Win, *Brock shares his strategies and success stories with yet another generation. If you have a special natural place or species of wildlife that you want to protect, Brock's principle "Endless pressure, endlessly applied" will surely inspire you to join this legendary eco-warrior in carrying the conservation movement forward with courage, wisdom, and persistence.*

Grammy-winning songwriter/performer/activist Carole King

This is no treatise on global warming, or the possibility of the extinction of polar bears. This is a book on "how to" effectively win your environmental cause. And no one can teach it better. And few people know that better than me. I have worked with him for years on "lost" causes that he won. Brock has done it time and time again. He is the Saul Alinsky of the environmental movement.

Sen. Robert Packwood, (R) Oregon

The American environmental movement has seen three evolutionary phases in its 120+ years—first we emphasized wilderness defense, then pollution control, and now climate change. Brock Evans has fought, led and won in all three realms, often simultaneously. His "operator's manual" preserves and refines the strategies and tactics that have served us best, and passes them on to the next generation in an accessible and intuitive style that makes this book a must-read for rising eco-fighters.

☙ **Sierra Club Director James Dougherty**

Brock Evans was an environmentalist long before that expression was coined. His book is part manifesto, part memoir, instructive yet engaging, a guide to save the earth by a man who has worked his entire life to do so. His tales and life stories are entirely applicable, grounded in the reality of how to make a difference, yet laced with humor that convinces his reader that conducting serious work can be fun, that the price of invested effort is well worth the victories that await. Evans motivates his readers to save the earth while handing them the blueprints and tools to do so. This is a must-read book for any environmentalist who has the fight in them to make a difference, and is willing to be led into battle for a righteous cause.

☙ **Writer/activist Colin Hodgkins**

Brock Evans is a superb advocate of people power in politics. Based on his own experience, he shows us how to get the right things done, and to come up smiling.

☙ **Wilderness author and educator Michael Frome**

To My Two Wonderful Muses

My Mother, Adele Erlandson
My Wife, Linda Garcia

Without whose gentle
"Endless Pressure Endlessly Applied"
this book could not have been completed.

Acknowledgments

This book has passed a long time inside my head and in my heart, rewritten over and over.

It was nearly a half century ago that I first discovered that all was not well in my beloved Northwest wilderness and ancient forests. Learning that other forces were out to destroy all that I had loved, I committed myself to trying to do something about it. Since that commitment, there has come a career—which itself has produced a torrent, a cascade of experiences, battles and campaigns and stories, now almost beyond count.

Now, even while heavily engaged in the campaigns of today, those past campaigns bubble up still from within, as a beautiful multi-colored tapestry of names and faces, excited voices and serious ones, hard times and good times, joys of victories, and the sadness of setbacks... a journey of rescuing our shared land that never ends—and must not end.

This book is about the lessons we have learned about how to succeed; and to remember:

1.   There were no environmental laws when we started out, in the 1960s, when nearly every wild and beautiful place— not to mention the air, water, and endangered species—was under assault from powerful economic interests.

2.   Now, 40 years later, several hundred million acres are protected by laws—enforceable laws; and all the strong environmental statutes like ESA are there too.

3.   Each one of those "green areas" on the map is there now, only because one person, or persons, loved them and cared enough to fight for them. Mostly unsung people, who gave unstintingly of themselves as volunteers for what they believed, and thus standing firm, ennobled themselves, by passing on these priceless places as permanent gifts to posterity.

Whenever I think about those campaigns from then until the present, a torrent of remembrances—of people—their names, faces and places, and their own individual stories, roils inside my head, saying: "tell me, please tell me, my story..."

These acknowledgements are in recognition of those remembrances, even now so acute; and of the wonderful people who made this book possible, either by their own direct efforts to save so much; or by encouraging me to continue, and to write down as much as I could when it was happening. For if we who were there do not do so, who will?

I must always start with Special Caregiver, wife Linda Garcia, who sacrificed much to nurse and care for me when I was stricken with "incurable" bone marrow cancer twelve years ago; and the same, a few years later, when a shattered shoulder immobilized me for months. There simply would not have been, could not have been, any book at all without such a life-partner. During the long book-gestation and writing process, Linda's suggestions, observations, and constant encouragement kept it all moving forward too.

My first conservation bosses at the Sierra Club, David Brower and Mike McCloskey, who hired me away from my law practice and mentored me early on... thus enabling a great blessing: to be able to spend my whole time from then henceforth doing what I loved—fighting for what I believed in, always alongside the many wonderful grassroots people, who were the heart and soul of each campaign and struggle. Strong national Club leaders who particularly inspired me, like Denny Shaffer, Phil Berry, Ted Snyder, Ed and Peggy Wayburn, Bill Futrell, Rebecca Falkenberry, Joni Bosh, Martin Litton, and so many others.

The names that follow are those whom I knew and worked with personally on the campaigns in this book, and in many other battles too. I know there are many others out there, whom I wish I knew better. To you I say thank you, blessings for what you have done and will do. It is so important; an essential part of our nation's soul depends on it.

So to the many past and present, unsung, personal comrades, remembered so clearly, still:

Alaska: Dixie Baade, Rich Gordon, C.H. Johnstone, Jack Calvin, George Longenbaugh, Peg Tileston, Andy Keller, Gershon Cohen.

Washington State: wilderness, parks and ancient forests: Pat Goldsworthy, Polly and John Dyer, Laura and Phil Zalesky, Emily Haig, Hazel Wolf, Raelene Gold, Frank Fickheisen, Bonnie Phillips, Judy Johnson, Bill Asplund, Jeb Baldi, Fred Darvill, Joan Thomas, Tom Wimmer, Jack Robertson, Lorna Smith, Susan Saul, Mitch Friedman, Karl Forsgaard, David Ortman, John Osborn, Rick McGuire, Jean and Marvin Durning, Tom and Mary Brucker, Elaine Packard, Chris Maykut, Sam Mace, Ray Kresek, Jay Holliday, Charlie Raines, Dave Knibb, Ben Hayes, Roger Mellem, Joe Scott, Norm Winn, Annette Tussing, Lunell Haught, Dave Fluharty, Marc Bardsley, George and Ann Mack, Dick Fiddler, Harry Lydiard, Tom Campion, Richard Rutz.

Oregon wilderness, parks, land use, ancient forests: Win and

Dick Noyes, Holway Jones, Sanford Tepfer, Larry Williams, Maradel Gale, Loren Hughes, Ken Witty, Ric Bailey, Jenn Williams, Charles Jones, Juanette Cremins, Darilyn Brown, Marilyn Cripe, Andy Kerr, Richard Gale, James Monteith, Michael Donnelly, Michael Houck, Dave Corkran, Cornelius Lofgren, Tim Lillebo, Joe Walicki, Jim Baker, Ellie Woods, Dave Willis, Wendell Wood, Carmelita Holland, John Rettig, Joan Zuber, Dominick DellaSalla, Nicole Cordan Ron Eber, Jack Barry, Dan Hall, Karen Anspacher-Meyer, and Ralf Meyer.

Idaho wilderness and rivers: Mort Brigham, Jerry Jayne, Boyd Norton, Jim Campbell, Pete Henault, Susan Drumheller, Rick Johnson, Tom Davis, Russ Brown, John Barker, Floyd Harvey, Pat and Bart Bartholomew, Russ Mager, Al McGlinsky.

Montana wilderness, rivers, and forests: Doris Milner, Guy Brandborg, Stuart Brandborg, Bill LaCroix, Patty Calcaterra, Loren Kreck, Dale Burke, Cecil Garland, Pat Antonick, Bill Cunningham, Derek Goldman, George Wuerthner, George Nikas, Deborah Richie, Matt Keohler, Larry Campbell, Cliff Merritt, Jeanette Russell, Kelsey Milner, Derek Goldman, Howie Wolke, Mike Bader.

Northern CA: Dave Vandemark, Winchell Hayward, Jan Randall, Mark Rockwell, Sarah Matsumoto, Felice Pace, Julia Levin.

Wyoming: Carroll Noble, Tom Bell, Jim Shore, Phil Hocker, Bart Koehler, Jim Kessler.

New Jersey: The saviors of Sparta Mountain: Phil and Sheryl Bishop, Anne Bowman, Wilma Frey... and the many children of community members who attended the hearings.

Washington, DC, fellow environmental workers for wilderness, land protections, endangered species and parks:

Ernie Dickerman, Art Wright, Fran Hunt, Mike Francis, Steve Holmer, Rodger Schlickeisen, Leda Huta, Marybeth Beetham, Bill Snape, Judy Noritake, Sharon Newsome, Tim Mahoney, Chuck Clusen, Bill Meadows, Jon Ellenbogen, Lisa Prickett, John Kostyack, Jay Hair, Brent Blackwelder, Rafe Pomerance, Linda Billings, Jim Dougherty, Cindy Shogan, Harriett Crosby, Don Barry, George Frampton, Marion Edey, Susan Holmes, Michael Leahy, Lee and Marty Talbot, Gilly Lyons, Marty Hayden, Deb Callahan, Beth Lowell, Susan Holmes, John McComb, Brooks Yeager, Mike Senatore, Jim Jontz, Paul Pritchard, Dave Alberswerth, Barbara Bramble, Destry Jarvis, Todd Tucci, Randi Spivak, Ron Tipton, Corey Westerbrook, Melissa Waage, Cynthia Wilson, Gwyn Jones, Jim Blomquist, Jim and Brenda Moorman, Jeff Norman, Chris Palmer, Kathy Robertson, Joe Browder, Hugh Youngblood, Brenda Mueller, Winsome MacIntosh, Loretta Neumann, Daphne Gemmel, Leslie Catherwood, Mitch Merry, Nancy Welch, Gwyn Jones, Bill Drayton, Lester Brown, Louise Dunlap, and Rich Nunno.

Other personal heroes across the U.S., true park/wilderness eco-warriors: Michael Kellett (MA), Lamar Marshall (AL), Doug Scott, Bill Arthur, Rachael Osborne, Peter Goldman, Peter Ilyn (WA), Michael Frome, Doug LaFollette, Michael Lehnert and Janette Marsh (WI), Laurie McDonald, Cynthia Frisch and Melissa Metcalfe (FL), Julie Gorte (NH), Tara Thornton, Jym St Pierre, Ken Spalding (ME), Roger Featherstone, Dinah Bear, Robin Silver, Peter Warshall, Michael Nixon (AZ), Mike Roselle (WVA), Laura Turner Seydel (GA), Clyde Gosnell (OH), Ollie Houck and Murray Lloyd (LA), Karin Heiman and Fred Stanback (NC), Ann Timberlake (SC) , Zach and Wendy Frankel (UT), Marge Sill (NV), Veronica Eagan, Tom Weiss, Tony Ruckel (CO), Liz Godfrey, Dave Forman, Nicole Rosemarino, Mark Salvo, Mat Jacobson (NM), Carole King, Carol Fulton, Ed Dobson, David Czamanske (CA), Pratt Remmel (AR), Jean Hocker, Rupert Cutler (VA), Mort Stelling (NE).

And strong National Audubon leaders and comrades such as Russ Peterson, Peter Berle, Glen Olson, Dan Taylor, Bob Turner, Walt Pomeroy, David Miller, Ron Klataske, Hope Babcock, Liz Raisbeck, Connie Mahan, Maureen Hinkle, Bill Butler, Norm Brunswig.

Native Americans: Suzanne Harjo, Levi Holt, Ola Cassadore, Mike Davis, Apache Nation, Lummi Nation, Nez Perce Nation.

Canada: Ric Careless and Dona Reel, Brian Vincent, Ken Farquardson (BC); Elizabeth May (Ontario), John Lammers (Yukon), Richard and Vivian Pharis, Diane Paschal (Alberta), First Nations of New Brunswick and British Columbia.

Across the Seas: Yoav Sagi, Robin Gordon, Alon Tal, Noam Gressel (Israel); Maria Hudakova (Slovakia), Andrei Laletin (Russia).

Special, longtime encouragers: Tim Greyhavens, Wilburforce Foundation; Jack Vanderryn, Moriah Fund; Mark Greene, American Heritage Center.

Major Muses over the past ten years: mother, Adele Erlandson, and wife Linda Garcia.

A special thank you to my wife Rachel, who was not only a great companion in those first years of exploring the Pacific Northwest and Alaska... but also a wonderful parent of our two sons during those early times when I had to travel across my vast PNW territory, and later, from Washington, DC—about fifty percent of the time. I adored my little boys, but if I could not travel, I could not do my job well, and could not add the experience to help others save their places. Rachel made all that possible.

Thank you to my amazing, savvy, enthusiastic, creative editors and marketers: Tina Bryan and John Campbell. What a wonderful team! Thanks too to their young colleagues Christine Stoddard of Quail Bell Press and editor/filmmaker William Bryan, and to book designer Jerri Anne Hopkins of Words & Pictures, Inc.

Finally but definitely not least, my colleagues and friends at Barclay Bryan Press and Campbell Communications join me in expressing heartfelt thanks to the scores of supporters, both friends and strangers, who've contributed money to the pro bono "Fight & Win" Campaign. Thanks to these generous comrades of ours, thousands of green high school and college students are receiving free copies of this book, in the hope that it will help them fight—and win.

More faces and voices keep nudging me inside, but at the moment I cannot quite connect with the names, and it is time to go.

But this list will not go; it will only grow... on and on, far into the future, as new people, with new ideas and new causes, step forward to carry on this wonderful people's movement. For that is really what it truly is, isn't it, this American Environmental Movement, which has so transformed America's landscapes, its air and waters? Transformed, in two generations, our whole sense of ourselves and who and just what we are as a Nation—one American people— forever united by these issues of our land and our love for it.

So when you take another look at a map someday, and notice again all those protected "green spaces"... never forget how they actually got there. And never forget where the love and the passion to save them always comes from.

That secret place, where they really came from, is to be found right inside each of us, in the hearts of the people themselves. Because, these struggles, battles, campaigns—they are not just tactical and strategic challenges, like some chess game.

What they really are is expressions of the human heart, and of our passion for our land.

I call them "Love Battles." And that is why we win so much, and will so continue.

So, to all of you, past, present and future eco-warriors out there, I say: thank you, and carry on. There is still much to do.

Brock Evans
Washington, DC
October 2013

Table of Contents

Introduction
HOW TO SAVE THE EARTH

This book is a practical manual on how to save and protect the natural places dear to us, large and small.

Grab a map and look at your town, your county, your state.

Look at all the patches of green. Most of these patches represent beautiful places and protected areas. And none of them was given protected status automatically or easily by some group of politicians or other decision-makers. Each one had to be fought for—by someone—to save it from being developed, and later to keep it from being developed.

Based on my decades of experience I can teach you specific strategies that will help you deal with huge corporate

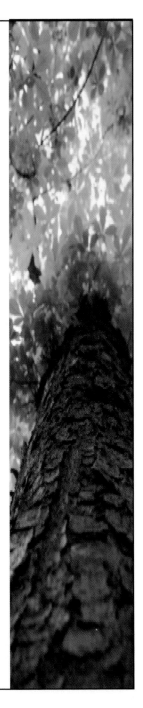

interests like big oil, big mining, and big timber. I can also show you how to win preservation fights on the local level.

As an environmental activist, you can't just go in with your fists swinging. You have to be smart. You need to know the angles. And I'm going to teach you what they are. I'll even throw in a few stories along the way. My main focus over the years has been on how ordinary people without any money can prevail over rich commercial interests—interests that are usually supported by politicians friendly to a given industry— to change people's minds, sometimes at the eleventh hour. I guarantee that studying how my colleagues and I have pulled off some unexpected preservation victories will put you and your allies way ahead of your opponents in any effort to preserve, protect, or clean up a specific vulnerable place.

And we all have to keep in mind that environmental events these days take place in the context of global climate change, the most critical problem we as humans will ever have to deal with. In addition, every single day more than a dozen plant and animal species go extinct because of habitat loss due to global warming and other human-activity-related phenomena. Science tells us that right now we're in an extinction era unprecedented since the demise of the dinosaurs. But it didn't have to get to this point; and it doesn't have to keep getting worse at the speeded-up rate that climatologists are now predicting.

I hope that you and some of the people you know are thinking about joining my friends and me in our ongoing, increasingly critical environmental battles. We badly need young advocates—now more than ever before. This is a book about how young people—and advocates of all ages—can save the land, air, and water, the plants and the creatures of this Earth—our only home, our precious and still-lovely planet.

Chapter One
THE SIX PRINCIPLES OF EFFECTIVE EARTH ACTION

The most consistent winners in the fight to save our natural environment have mastered what I call the Six Principles of Effective Earth Action. These principles are absolutely key to our successes. They guide us to make the most effective use of resources at hand. And they help us maintain the perspective we need to win, even when things get discouraging.

Principle 1: Don't be afraid.

Your opposition might outnumber you. They might have more money, more power, more self-assurance.

They might tell you that you don't know what you're doing. They might accuse you of standing in the way of economic progress and job creation.

Be polite, but don't listen.

Some powerful interests are afraid of young, passionate people. It's because they know that you, too, have power, and can mess things up for them.

You have the power to organize your friends using the new technologies, of whipping up fast grassroots support in ways that were never possible before. You have the power to shape public opinion and to influence legislation. And you tend to have more energy and a far deeper aptitude for commitment than they or their people ever will.

It's okay for people to disagree with you. What matters is that you stick to your goals. Don't let the opposition frighten you, or cause you to hold back. Simply refuse to be intimidated or discouraged.

Principle 2: Conservation is politics.

Not party politics, as in Republican and Democrat (although that can make a difference sometimes, too). What I mean here is that the final decision to save a particular place or to clean up a polluted waterway is always made by someone other than the developer or property owner; the real decision-makers are on the County Council or the regional commission or in the state or federal legislature. These people are either elected officials or appointed officials whose duty it is to listen to, and respond to, the elected ones. And they can't act completely arbitrarily; they have to follow rules.

If a project is being pursued by developers using their own money (generally money borrowed from a bank), they still have to get permits from the decision-makers and follow environmental laws regarding pollution and land use. Plus, the developers have to persuade the lenders that this project will make money for them. Studying the politics of your situation can also guide your strategy from the start in some wonder-fully effective ways. Let's say a developer can't get final approval for his project until the public has had a chance to weigh in at a public hearing. The hear-ing is scheduled and publicized. Your group, though, isn't ready to present your case as persuasively as you know you could if only you had a little more time—you don't have all your data collected yet, let's suppose. You need to buy time.

Find out the formal framework in which the hearing is mandated to operate, and see if you can tweak it to your advantage.

The story that follows is about a time we succeeded through (a) knowing and playing by the governmental

rules, and (b) taking advantage of politicians' great vulnerability, their fear of making the public mad. The tactic bought us the time we needed to get our campaign in fighting trim.

⮞ The place that was threatened was up in the mountains of northern New Jersey. Our group lived in cottages around a small lake, nestled into the side of a big mountain. We cherished our peace and quiet on Sparta Mountain, and we cherished our neighbors—the bears, deer, herons, and wild turkeys—who shared the lake and its surrounding deep forests with us.

But one summer our group learned that a wealthy developer had plans to tear down the forests and rare wetlands of the mountainside in order to construct a massive vacation-home subdivision and golf course.

"This is awful," said one of my friends. "Not only will it destroy the habitat of some rare and endangered species that live here, the noise and traffic and lights will completely destroy the peace and quiet of nature, which we've loved so long here."

"Yeah, but what can we do about it?" said another neighbor. "It's a done deal. The developer has it all wired. The Zoning Board is going to hold a final approval hearing next week, and this rich guy has all the right friends in high places. He'll get what he wants."

"Oh, really?" I said. "How big is the hearing room?"

My friends looked at me as if I were crazy. What difference did the size of the hearing room make? The whole proceeding was rigged anyway—a done deal. All the developer needed was final approval.

"Well, maybe it's not impossible," I said. "Let's go down today and take a look."

We drove down the mountain into the town and looked in the conference room they'd advertised for the hearing. It was small, and looked like it could hold only twenty to thirty people.

"Okay," I said. "Here's our strategy for next week. The developer may think he has this wired, but he doesn't have one strength that we can come up with: ordinary people. I bet we can easily get up to two hundred folks to show up for this so-called final approval hearing. Can't we?"

"Maybe, but what's the point? They won't be able to get into the room."

"That's the whole point," I said. "When so many of us show up, demanding to get in, and we can't, the Zoning Board will panic. They're obliged by law to let the community have its say. They'll have to cancel and reschedule the hearing for another day in a bigger room, which will give us time to organize and get stronger. We all hate this development plan, so let's start fighting back—now!"

And that's what we did.

We went to work and asked a lot of people, and nearly one hundred of them showed up—and made a show of trying to cram into that tiny room. Of course it was impossible. The Zoning Board was startled; they'd had no idea the plan was so controversial! They canceled the hearing on the spot and rescheduled it for a month later in the town auditorium.

By then we were ready. We had formed an organization, Friends of Sparta Mountain. We'd written, and sent out, hundreds of flyers and alerts, urging people to come to the newly rescheduled hearing and speak up. We'd sent out "citizen ambassadors" to visit other lakeside communities in the area and plead for their support. And we'd prepared and distributed a colorful and detailed document outlining a new plan—to establish the same wild mountainside as an official Protected Area.

And our new allies did come to the auditorium— hundreds of them! That show of strength and opposition really stopped the whole project dead in its tracks. There were more hearings later, but we kept getting stronger in numbers and more outspoken.

Finally the developer gave up.

He sold his land to the State of New Jersey. And since then, those bears, deer, wild turkeys, coyotes, owls, and herons have lived peacefully and safely in their 3,200-acre Sparta Mountain State Wildlife Management Area.

Principle 3: Persistence is everything.

Some of those green areas on the map took years of campaigning to protect. Others took only a few weeks.

No matter how long it takes, you must see it to the end. And here's something else: your opposition must become convinced, beyond the slightest doubt, that you're going to see it to the end. Persistence is one of your most powerful weapons. In the long run it's very difficult, often impossible, for an opponent to handle.

This doesn't mean you can't take a break from the campaign; but you may want to reconsider your schedule. Or if you find out that key decision-makers are coming out to look at your target site, or want to have a meeting on a day when you're unavailable, make sure one of your trusted allies steps in for you. Your opponents have to know that the campaign is your group's top priority and that you're never going to quit, even if, as individuals, you have occasional distractions.

At first, of course, they'll assume that you'll fight for a while and eventually get tired and depressed and go away. They'll spend their time and money opposing you, and consider it worthwhile.

But one wonderful day it will dawn on them that you're never, literally never, going to quit. Then they'll be forced to question whether you're really worth fighting. Maybe they won't want to go through all the trouble, expense—and bad publicity, if that's starting to happen —of continuing to push their project. At some point they'll probably decide to change their plans or give up altogether. It's absolutely key to winning advocacy battles: persistence.

In our campaigns, it's always The Other Side who gives up. Believe me.

Principle 4: Start early and nail down the facts as fast as you can.

Too often, we wake up to find beloved areas gone.

We don't even know that a place is doomed until the bulldozers and chainsaws arrive. While it's not im-possible even then to save the place (and there are note-worthy examples of this I'll tell you about), it's much, much easier to succeed if you can start taking action early.

Never assume that just because every-one loves a place it will be there forever. Recognize that in these times of fast (and often destructive) change, the special place you value is not safe, unless it's explicitly been designated a protected area.

So how do you begin the process of finding out what's happening, or will happen, to a place you care about?

Be on the lookout for a sign in your neighborhood that says "Lot for Sale" or "Future Site of [Whatever]." Start asking people about it. Ask your neighbors, ask people who work in the area, ask local environmentalists.

Here are the questions to ask:

1. What are they planning to do here?
2. When are they planning to do it?
3. Who's doing it?
4. Do you know them?
5. Which government department or official has to approve the project?
6. If a permit has already been given to the developer, which bank has approved (or has to approve) the loan?

The vital thing is to find out all you can, as quickly as you can, and the two most important questions are Numbers 1 and 2, regarding what and when. What exactly is being planned, and for when? Don't lose a minute getting the fundamental facts, and then double- and triple-check to make sure your information is reliable.

One of those facts you dig up is going to resonate particularly with the community. Don't expect a strong emotional response to a whole menu of particulars when time is short—focus, if you can, on publicizing one particularly alarming fact that will get people's attention.

The park was next door to an elementary school and contained a playground. A group calling itself a "Citizens' Committee" decided that most of the trees in the park were about to fall down and so posed a health and safety hazard for the children. (Besides, these committee folks thought the trees were ugly. How much nicer, they said, for the children to have grassy expanses with flowers and shrubs and an otherwise more manicured environment.)

This committee asked the City Council to "improve" the park, starting by cutting all the trees down and landscaping the property. The Parks Department loved the idea, of course, because grass-covered open space is so much cheaper and easier to maintain than a woodsy park with natural groves of trees.

Nobody talked to the people who used the park daily. It was easy for the Parks Department to decide that this "Citizen's Committee's" proposal should be implemented. Since this was all they'd heard on the subject, the Department could pretend that this is what the public wanted (or, beyond that, that the public didn't care). They held two quiet meetings—minimally publicized— in those tiny little conference rooms.

EMERGENCY!

ALL THE TREES IN FINLAY PARK & PLAYGROUND ARE SCHEDULED TO BE CUT DOWN

by our Parks & Recreation Dept.
but with your help, we can stop this destruction!

Come to a public hearing and tell Parks & Rec.
NO to cutting down OUR trees!

When: THURSDAY, MARCH 21, 1:30pm
Where: Fourth Street Community Center
No more hearings are scheduled. This will be our ONLY
CHANCE to save Finlay Park's trees. Please join us!

For information call (306) 555-9898
Friends of Finlay Park & Playground

Fortunately we local folk found out (almost by accident) just in the nick of time. A neighbor happened to over-hear someplace that all the trees were scheduled to come down, and that the final parks meeting was to take place in ten days' time!

Clearly there was no time to mount a full-scale cam-paign. There was barely time to act at all, though we had to. But how? We found out that no one else in the neighborhood had heard about the park "improvement" plan either. It was time to get nimble and creative, fast, so that everyone heard about it!

We concentrated on a ten-block radius around the park. We had time for only one quick meeting, in somebody's living room one spring night. We'd gath-ered together a small group—seven adults and two teenagers. Together we decided that launching a flyer campaign was the way to go.

It was the fact we'd found out that "ALL our trees are going to be CUT DOWN" that hit the community's nerve. Most people like trees. No other aspects of the project needed to be mentioned at this point.

We had 3,000 copies of the flyer printed, and recruited our kids and our friends to help distribute them. The teenagers on our committee collected a whole army of high school kids to join in. We divided up who was going to take what street, and we went door to door through the whole ten-block area. We knocked on every door, handed people the flyer, and asked them

to come to the meeting on Thursday of the following week—and emphasized that it was now or never! Then we waited.

We almost held our breaths out of nervousness as the day of the public hearing rolled around. Would people come or not? Would we succeed in saving our park's trees or not?

We needn't have worried.

Before the meeting even started there were at least a thousand people there. By the time it was over there were almost two thousand people at the Community

Center saying "NO!" to the tree-cutting scheme. The Parks Department officials, astonished at the huge number of residents who opposed their plan, of course voted not to go forward.

More than thirty-five years later the park and its trees are still safe. Often when I walk by I'll give a hug to an old mulberry tree (opposite page), still spreading its shady branches and providing shelter to birds, insects, and animals. That old friend had been the number-one target of the chainsaws, incidentally, because the committee thought it "looked messy." ༄

Principle 5: Craft a killer message

Your official message is the beating heart of your campaign.

Maybe you'll have to brainstorm for days to hit upon the perfect message; or maybe it will strike one of you, suddenly, like a flash of genius out of the blue, in the first minute of your first organizational meeting.

Your message is your single most important weapon of all.

The message is a short, memorable phrase that will make others—potential allies, the public, the decision-makers—suddenly see things from your point of view, even if they disagree. It's also a reinforcing tool for keeping your own team's emotional momentum up—marching forward, themselves (and you too), even when everyone starts feeling discouraged. (And you will experience some terribly discouraging times, it's guaranteed. Better plan on it.)

Sometimes the message consists of only a few words; at the most it's a sentence. The message makes it clear, right away, why this place is of value and should be protected or restored.

The trick is to come up with the shortest, yet the most positively stated (and accurate) few words that will plant the seed psychologically; that on an emotional level will spark the reaction you want to evoke. Make sure that your key phrase is embodied in almost everything you communicate to the public, and that it's one that resonates.

When we started those campaigns in Oregon to save the forests with the biggest trees, we knew we couldn't have our message be, "Please save these forests because they're so beautiful." That's because much of the economy of Oregon depended—or at least people thought it did—on cutting down all the huge trees we were trying to protect. (That wasn't really true, but it was a "political fact" that many people believed at the time.)

We quickly learned that neither newspaper editors nor most in the general public would respond to the "because they're so beautiful" message. But they might respond positively if they knew that these huge trees that they were taking for granted were biologically and historically unique. So a small group of us got together and spent a day asking ourselves: "What is it, what is so special about these forests? How can we tell in just a few words what they really are and why they're so precious?"

And we came up with two great words that say it all. ***Ancient Forests.***

We said, "That's our message, because that's the true essence of what they really are, and why they're so rare and valuable. These forests are Nature's masterpieces—forests of giant trees, hundreds, some even thousands of years old. Hundreds and thousands of years old, it's incredible! There are only a few left, and they must be protected for all future generations to have and enjoy."

That phrase, "ancient forests"—our message—worked beautifully and gained us a lot of support. A number of influential people suddenly saw the point, and joined us. ᐁ

Principle 6: Endless pressure, endlessly applied

If you and your group keep at it, you're eventually going to win, or at least shape the outcome in major and decisive ways. It's as simple as that.

Developers and decision-makers are not prepared to overcome the force of endless pressure endlessly applied.

I'll repeat this. ***If you commit yourself wholeheartedly to endless pressure endlessly applied, you'll succeed.***

By "endless pressure" I mean never letting up, and doing something every day to advance your cause. It can be writing a daily post or blog, or making one phone call. Other days it will be speaking at a hearing or sending a letter to the editor of the local paper. Other times it will be handing out flyers in mall parking lots. And other times it may mean arguing (constructively) with your own coalition members.

Keep your pressure points in mind, though—the decision-makers who need to give final approval to the proposed project—and keep the pressure on in both direct and indirect ways.

Remember that a priceless byproduct of endlessly and actively pressuring the decision-makers is that you'll probably start to get publicity, and soon the public will take your cause seriously—they'll feel that they've heard about this problem for so long, it must be important! And one thing decision-makers care about, in most cases, is what the public thinks. Endless pressure endlessly applied on decision-makers by your group can turn into final pressure applied on them by a public who's become impressed, over time, with your commitment and your message.

~ Whenever I think about the principle "endless pressure, endlessly applied," I remember a lovely place called French Pete Creek, out in Oregon. French Pete Creek (named after an old sheepherder years ago) was actually a large valley, and it was chock full of huge trees, many of them hundreds of years old.

But there was a problem: the whole valley was scheduled to be logged, because these enormous trees were so valuable as lumber, and because the timber industry there and then was so powerful.

Politically, no one dared to challenge them. Back in those days the logging companies always got what they wanted.

Indeed, so successful and unchallenged were the timber companies that almost every other valley in the entire state had already been stripped of its giant trees. These valleys, consequently, couldn't provide decent habitat for the fish and animals that once lived there, or anything for human recreation or enjoyment.

I heard about the plight of French Pete Creek from Oregon friends. They were despondent because the timber industry was too mighty a foe. My friends complained that the decision-makers wouldn't listen to them.

"We've tried, and asked, and pleaded with them, two times before —and both times they said no."

I refused to believe that there was no way at all. There had to be some way. So I went down to visit, and they took me on a hike through the forest. It was one of the most beautiful places I'd ever seen.

At a meeting that night I persuaded my friends to start a new campaign, one in which we'd simply refuse to take no for an answer. Period. If the officials said no again, and said it again and again and again and again, we'd just keep coming back and trying harder. I knew the decision-makers would eventually have to say yes.

This brave group of Oregonians knew that their neighbors would be mad at them and the papers would criticize them for standing in the way of "progress" (jobs and increased revenues for the state); and they worried about all the time and work the campaign would demand of them. But they agreed.

"Okay," they said, "we're in. And we're in it to the finish. We won't give up this time, ever."

And so they went back to work to save their valley. They publicized pictures of the beautiful place, they placed ads in the papers, they demanded (and got) public hearings, they knocked on doors, and they organized their neighbors to come and speak out. They even went to court to get a delay in the implementation of the logging plan.

Because of this endless pressure endlessly applied, the timber interests finally gave up. They could foresee having to fight it out forever, and they didn't want to get stuck doing that.

Today French Pete—the whole valley, with its magnificent ancient forests—is part of a Federal Wilderness Area.

Endless pressure, endlessly applied.

Chapter Two
PUTTING YOUR CAMPAIGN TOGETHER

Start by recruiting your team.

It may be only one friend, but I hope it's at least a handful of like-minded people who know that defeating your greedy, nature-destroying opponents —whether they be an individual wealthy developer and his associates or a planning council or a land-owning institution (like a university looking to expand its buildings and parking lots) or a commercial mining company—is going to take time and work. And that your opponents might be hostile, even aggressive, and try their best to

31

make you look and feel bad, with the assumption that you'll quit.

I hope everyone in your group will recognize that it's vitally important to be brave; that persistence is everything; that you can make politics work for you; that if you start early and learn all you can as quickly as you can your chances of success are great; that a fantastic message is going to be one of your most powerful weapons; and that endless pressure, endlessly applied, wins the day.

Here are a few things you'll need to have in place before you can take action. I call them your Campaign Toolbox.

1. Headquarters

Of course you'll be making maximum use of Facebook, Twitter, texting, and the phone, but please convince your crew that there's no substitute for meeting face to face—regularly. Your HQ can be your kitchen or basement or a friend's living room or a conference room at the public library or your nearest coffee shop. But don't think that a successful campaign can be waged exclusively online via email, social networking, or texting. It can't. As vital as communications technology is going to be in your effort, there's no substitute for meeting in person—and often.

Study after study has shown that people feel happiest and most motivated to give of themselves when they feel that they're part of a cause greater than themselves. This is because of the power of bonding. Bonding cannot be achieved through the electronic exchange of information alone; it has to be done through personal interaction.

2. Supplies

Notebooks. Stuff to write with. Folders to keep things organized. Remember that you're going to be generating a lot of paper documents (flyers, letters) even in this electronic age, and you need to keep track of them all, with dates on when a certain piece was printed up, when and where distributed, and so on. You'll also need to file away every bit of paper that comes your way during the campaign (like angry letters from your opponent). In practical and legal terms, paper still rules.

3. Equipment

Whatever communications equipment you already have and are comfortable with (tablet, phone, laptop). Have cameras or else phones with picture- and/or video-taking capacity (you'll be taking lots and lots of pictures). The researcher in your group will of course need frequent access to the Internet. You should also have a color printer (or access to one) and presentation software such as Photoshop or InDesign.

Chapter Three

TWELVE TIPS ON GETTING YOUR CAMPAIGN OFF ON THE RIGHT FOOT

These tips are all guaranteed to start your campaign strong, and keep it running effectively. Implement them in the order that feels most useful to you.

TIP #1: Give your place and your campaign a name.

Deciding this will be very similar to crafting your message. The name should describe what you're doing, and be memorable. For example, if it's a woods in your neighborhood, you might call your campaign "Save Clairmont Neighborhood Forest."

Even if your campaign name lends itself to a catchy acronym—if you're calling your group "Bowes-Rapidan Valley Environmentalists," say, which your team might be tempted to refer to as BRAVE—remember that most abbreviations and acronyms are impersonal, cold, technical. Words themselves are personal, warm, and easy for folks to relate to.

Example: the famous Arctic National Wildlife Refuge in Alaska, which oil companies are always trying to open up for drilling. Oil company supporters always call this seventeen-million-acre wilderness by its initials—ANWR, pronounced "Anwar"—because they know this name is cold, meaningless in itself, and foreign-sounding. We environmentalists are always careful to say the whole thing slowly: "Arctic... National...Wildlife...Refuge," because each word really drives home the reality and significance of this amazing and beautiful place.

TIP #2: Make sure everyone agrees to hold regular, brief, in-person meetings.

The most important reason for your group to meet at regular intervals is psychological. Coming together on a regular basis as a group, in person, is essential.

If you just have one kick-off meeting and then stay in communication with each other through texting, phone, email, or any other way—even if the one-to-one "conversations" are constant—your coalition will grow weak and continue to get weaker, *and one or two people will end up doing all the thinking and working.* Keep your meetings to-the-point so that they're brief and useful. But keep holding them.

A recent study of enlisted men in the Army showed that soldiers in combat say their number-one motivation to keep going is not patriotism or dedication to the cause or respect for their commanding officers. It's the desire not to let their brothers down. The bonds between these people who've shared danger and hardship on behalf of a common objective is a source of power—for each of them individually and for their unit.

Your campaign to save a wild mountain valley from being flooded by a new dam may not be war, but the concrete benefits of camaraderie and being there for each other still apply.

TIP #3: Use maps.

There's a magic and a power to boundaries, and they engage the human imagination. It's far more effective to see the clearly labeled Eagle Mountain Refuge with a line around it, on a map or an aerial photo, than to hear the description "the nine hundred acres on Eagle Mountain north of Lake Onslow and southwest of Chips Creek." Draw a thick boundary line around your area on a map, and post it in your headquarters space so everyone sees it at every meeting.

Make a map for public distribution too. Everyone knows what happens when a woodland or farm or park gets replaced by an office building or Walmart or some other money-making, man-made facility: the area around it inevitably gets developed, too. Create a map showing what could happen to the whole area—not just your special place—once the development ball gets rolling. You might even do a little research and discover that plans already exist for local government to rezone or otherwise facilitate development in the wider area. People need to know this! When they do they might join forces with your group to save the whole area before development gets out of hand.

TIP #4: Make someone your group's official researcher

Ask someone who's smart and careful and good at Internet research to take charge of information gathering and fact checking.

There are few things more awful than confidently citing facts and figures in a public hearing or a lobbying session, only to be corrected (especially if it's your opponent doing the correcting). Not only is this embarrassing—you and your whole campaign risk losing credibility. Someone should have the regular job of going online to gather up-to-date information, and also to check "facts" that your group has heard and takes to be true— but that should be verified anyway, just in case.

Your researcher should also check out the information on which the opposition bases its arguments. Sometimes your opponents might be misinformed, or not up to date on changing data. Sometimes they're lying. A good researcher should be open-minded but a bit cynical.

Sometimes the enemy's "facts" are accepted by virtually everybody as the truth—even you and your comrades!—when actually they're not true at all. I've been in situations in which we thought, "Well, we can't use Strategy A because of XYZ situation, so let's come up with a Strategy B that might work instead," and then eventually found that everyone was wrong about XYZ in the first place. As I've said, sometimes the opposition lies outright, sometimes they bend the truth. Sometimes they sincerely believe that their flawed data are correct.

☙ I'm reminded of the story of the saving of Horseshoe Basin back in 1967. This is a beautiful 20,000-acre piece of land at the far eastern edge of the North Cascades, up near the Canadian border in the state of Washington. It was once a part of the North Cascades Primitive Area, but as the North Cascades parks legislation was going through Congress this chunk of land was always omitted from the maps. I asked why.

"We can't save Horseshoe Basin for you because it has too much timber on it," came back the answer. "One hundred million board feet."

Wow. That's a lot of timber.

On the Fourth of July weekend my wife and I and several friends went over to Horseshoe Basin to take a

look. We found a lovely, high, rolling meadow country with little streams dancing through it and tremendous views of the great chain of peaks that are the North Cascades. We had a glorious time among the flowers, high up there in the sun.

What about all that timber? We didn't see it. The trees

were mostly scraggly lodgepoles, with some big trees near creek bottoms, but that was about it.

When I got back to my office I directed a lengthy letter to the Forest Supervisor, asking where all this timber was. I requested that he be very specific—place by place, drainage by drainage.

The Supervisor was a straight shooter. When he got my letter he asked his timber staff to do a "recruise," meaning a very detailed re-examination of every place I'd named.

Sometime shortly after Labor Day I received the Supervisor's response: "We did a recruise and found that our original estimate of one hundred million board feet was in error. There is only eighteen million board feet of commercial timber there."

This was powerful new information! But what to do with it?

Hearings had already been held in the Senate, and I knew that the Interior Committee was going to act soon and report out a bill.

Was there still time?

I called up Bill Van Ness, chief staffer on this issue for Senator Henry Jackson of Washington, Chairman of the Committee. Whatever Senator Jackson wanted to be in the bill affecting his state would be there, I knew. I was almost afraid to make the call—maybe I was too late and we had lost Horseshoe Basin already. Nobody had ever even mentioned it during any of the hearings. I screwed up my courage and dialed anyway.

"When are you guys going to mark up the North Cascades legislation?" I asked.

"We've scheduled it for Monday." And this was Friday!

I worked my way into the subject by asking about other things first. "Can you tell me what the Committee is going to do about . . . the Park, the Glacier Peak region . . ." etc.

I got good affirmative answers. Finally I popped the question.

"What about Horseshoe Basin?"

"Oh, we're leaving that one out of the Wilderness, Brock. Too much good commercial timber, and the mill at Omak needs it."

I asked him to hang on for a minute and read him the letter I'd just gotten from the Forest Service.

It had its effect on Bill. After a pause he said, "Can you get this letter to us by Monday?"

I rushed it down to SeaTac airport—this was in the days before FedEx and fax machines—and mailed it off, Airmail Special Delivery. All weekend I just hoped and hoped.

I arrived at the office Monday about nine, knowing that because of the three-hour time difference they might well have marked the legislation up already. Perhaps the fate of Horseshoe Basin was already decided. I had come to love that magical faraway place, just cared too much about it by then.

Finally I could stand waiting no longer—got Bill on the phone.

"Hi, Bill, this is Brock. Is the markup over, and can you tell me what the Committee did?" Nervously I decided to ask about other places first. "What about the Suiattle and its tributaries Buck Creek and Downey Creek?" (Huge trees there.)

"We put 'em in."

"What about the Stehekin?"

"It's a Recreation Area, but no logging. Same with Granite Creek."

Finally, "What about Horseshoe Basin?"

"Oh yes, Brock. We got your letter. Thanks. The Committee put it back in the Wilderness."

I've never forgotten the relief I felt. Nor have I forgotten the lessons learned then—recheck the "facts" upon which the opposition is basing its own efforts; and use what you learn as quickly and effectively as you can. Information is power, and if delivered to the right people at the right time, it can be enormously forceful. It's been thirty years since I've wandered in that high country of lakes, rolling meadows, and forested stream valleys. But the joy I feel every time I see its name on the map—inside that green line —is simply indescribable. ❧

I hope your researcher will also do background snooping on your opponents and their plans and track records. Even more important is doing background research on officials with whom you're going to meet. Knowing as much as you can ahead of time about the big fish you're trying to persuade—his or her likes, dislikes, hobbies, personal prejudices and enthusiasms and aversions—is one of the lobbyist's most cherished strategies.

I remember a very important meeting which we almost botched because we hadn't done the proper research into our official's personal life. We rescued it at the last minute, but only because we were lucky.

My little group was working very hard to persuade the U.S. Congress to pass legislation to protect all the remaining ancient forests in the Pacific Northwest.

We had maneuvered the bill through two very tough subcommittees, over the fierce opposition of the timber industry. The next day was going to be the critical one: the vote of the full committee. If we could persuade enough members of Congress to vote with us, we'd likely have clear sailing to get a good result when it came to the House floor for a vote.

So we got appointments with four or five key Congresspeople who sat on the committee and would have a vote, but who hadn't committed themselves yet. It was terribly important that they hear our case and decide to vote with us.

Our small group split up the members to visit. My friend Tom and I were assigned to see a Congressman from a Midwestern state.

It was about six o'clock in the evening at the end of a very busy day. We were shown into the office of the conspicuously busy Congressman. He was clearly distracted and impatient; he was polite enough, but kept drumming his fingers on his desk and looking at his watch, not really listening. It was clear he just wanted us to get out of there.

But what to do? We couldn't just leave it like that! He wouldn't know, much less care, anything about these forests we'd come so far to protect. He just wasn't listening, and was answering in monosyllables, if at all. Totally not interested.

In my heart I was resigned to the disaster of a failed meeting. "That's the way it goes sometimes," I thought. "Win some, lose some."

My friend Tom squirmed in his chair awkwardly, desperately glancing around the room, not wanting to leave matters in such a bad spot. Then his eyes lighted on a picture hanging right over the Congressman's desk. It showed ducks coming in to land on a lovely marshland.

"Oh, I just noticed that picture, Congressman," he said. "Are those wood ducks?"

"Yes, they are. Do you know ducks?"

"Well, yes! I love to go hunting at home. I love the whole experience. Wood ducks are especially beautiful."

The Congressman perked up, no doubt relieved that the subject was changing.

"Me, too. I live for it whenever I go home on recess.

What's your favorite . . .?"

And the conversation picked up, taking a very lively turn about ducks—forget the big trees for the moment! No matter. All of a sudden he was no longer looking at his watch or drumming his fingers. He was engaged, liking it all.

After a little while of this the Congressman said, "Now tell me again, why are you guys here?"

We told him again about the ancient forests.

"And the vote is tomorrow. How do you want me to vote?"

"With us, in favor of the bill, sir," said the Congressman's new duck-hunting friend Tom.

"Fine. Done. Thank you for coming in," he smiled as he escorted us to the door. ⟡

TIP #5: Go for diversity in your group.

I'm not thinking about racial or ethnic or religious diversity here, though this remains an important unmet challenge for the environmental movement as a whole.

I'm talking about ideological diversity.

Some people have the completely erroneous idea that all the most passionate environmentalists are upper-middle-class, politically "progressive," pacifist kinds of folks, who'd never vote for anyone but a liberal Democrat. If this describes you, that's fine, only please don't make the mistake of seeking support just from the politically like-minded. Reach out to everyone who cares about our precious environment.

Though there are plenty of left-leaning people in the ranks of eco-warriors, young and old, there are legions of people whose political orientation is very conservative. Among the most effective heroes in our battles to protect forests, rivers, lakes, the atmosphere, and all other components of the wild natural ecosphere are hunters, fishermen, and other lovers of outdoor recreation. How any such randomly selected persons would vote on gay marriage or abortion or immigration policy is entirely irrelevant, and how you would vote on such issues is equally of no interest or importance.

I am a proud U.S. Marine Corps veteran. I don't say "former Marine" because once you're a Marine you're a Marine for life. *Semper fi!*

Since the Salmo Valley was all located on public land, I decided to write to the official in charge of that National Forest, Supervisor Bob Smart. Smart turned out to be a good man, a straight shooter, and he was willing to answer all my questions.

In my letter I introduced myself as someone working with the Sierra Club and politely asked if the Forest

Service had any particular plans to build roads or cut trees in the Salmo Valley.

Mr. Smart wrote back quickly, and in a friendly tone. "Yes, we have a good plan for the Salmo Valley. Next year we're going to punch a logging road down to the bottom so we can cut the trees and get them to a sawmill. Then we plan to put recreational campgrounds next to the logging roads and clearcuts."

Well, I thought to myself, I was right—this is a place full of precious ancient forests, still untouched. And they're going to log it. Our problem is that no one knows about this place. At least no one I know knows about it. What to do? The place is three hundred miles away. I couldn't save it by myself even if I tried. I had to find friends and allies who'd help.

The first step in putting together a group of allies in those days (pre-Internet) was getting out my mailing lists. I paid particular attention to the lists for the city of Spokane—the largest city nearest to the Salmo.

I sent a letter to the five or six conservation leaders I could identify in that area. I didn't know them personally, but reasoned that they would be sympathetic.

Little did I know what would happen after that! My letter to each of them simply enclosed copies of the correspondence between me and Mr. Smart...and I said, "This Salmo River seems like a pretty nice place, worth protecting. Do you know it?"

It turned out that all of them knew a lot about it—and one person especially, Ray Kreseck, loved the place. Ray was a fireman with the Spokane City Fire Department. He loved to go hunting and fishing deep down inside the little remote wilderness valley of the Salmo. He was outraged to learn that there were plans to log it and cart the great forests off to a sawmill.

Ray took action.

The next thing I knew, hundreds of letters to Mr. Smart started to pour out of the city of Spokane—from hunters and fishermen, all friends of Ray's, all of whom knew and loved the Salmo River valley.

These letter-writers made it clear they were passionate about the place just as it was, and demanded that no logging take place.

As soon as I saw that flood of letters from Ray and his friends I knew that we had a real campaign going. I would help them all I could, and I did; but they were the leaders. Under their guidance we worked very hard, writing more letters, going to public meetings, talking with decision-makers.

It took several years, but we won.

Now that little valley (and an equally beautiful one next to it) is safe forever. It's known as the Salmo-Priest Wilderness Area, and it's 41,000 acres of gorgeous ancient forest and rivers and a beautiful lake.

TIP # 6: Embrace the public hearing.

A public hearing is a fantastic tool. If the decision-making authorities relevant to your project haven't scheduled public hearings on your issue yet, make sure they do. Citizens have a right to be heard.

A public hearing is open to everyone. All residents can voice their opinions about the matter at hand. The local governing body will be obligated to listen, and to consider these opinions before making its decisions.

An important bonus: hearings are automatic media opportunities. Reporters and cameras are often in the hearing room. My colleagues and I often hold a press conference thirty minutes before the hearing's start time. Be sure to bring plenty of printed copies of your press release, and come prepared to deliver a couple of good sound bites on camera.

Don't be nervous or afraid about public hearings. They're golden opportunities. Believe me, the developer would far rather skip these hearings. He'd always prefer to deal quietly, alone, with the decision-makers—because in a hearing, ordinary people are given a chance to speak out, and it's their best (and

sometimes only) chance to derail an unpopular development or resources-exploiting project.

There are three main reasons that public hearings are your best friend:

1. Hearings allow you to demonstrate that your proposal has a lot of support. "Look how many people took time off work to come speak out for protecting those woods!" is what the decision-makers will be thinking. There's always strength in numbers.

2. Attending hearings makes it easier for you find and gather more allies.

3. Hearings make you distill your most powerful message and arguments. You'll use them to reach as many people as possible: through email, snail mail, flyers, and (most importantly) face-to-face contact. Most people are best persuaded by face-to-face communication, of course, and that's what a hearing is a forum for.

What frequently happens at public hearings is that minds get changed. New facts and arguments are brought to light, and the decision-makers listen. They're persuaded by the physical presence, the body language and passion of the people who come to speak.

Don't ever let yourself stay home instead of attending a public hearing, unless it's really a matter of life and death. I've said before that the public hearing is your best friend, and it's true. To decision-makers

a citizen's appearance at a hearing is more important than a personal letter. Why? Because everyone
knows it's a bother to go to a hearing. It's even harder
to speak out. It's also a lot of trouble to get dressed
up properly and to spend the time to get yourself
down to the hearing room without losing your nerve
or deciding that your presence really isn't going to
be necessary to the cause after all. The whole thing
takes courage. Everyone knows that you'll encounter
opposition, even hostility and shouting.

Decision-makers know this and respect the person

who does it, and accordingly will tend to pay attention to that person's concerns. Don't worry about looking or sounding nervous! Nervousness can actually work to your advantage; people always sympathize with stage fright, and you'll come off as authentic rather than polished.

TIP #7: Get people over to your place.

This has worked again and again. We had a regular program, for instance, of bringing members of Congress from Eastern states out into the Pacific Northwest, just to walk among the giant forests. There's all the difference in the world between hearing about a place's value and actually seeing the place with one's own eyes.

This one activity has been practically can't-miss for us; once the decision-makers and their families see the ancient trees, sparkling clean rivers, and indigenous animals, birds, and fish, we know they'll probably vote to save the places.

TIP #8: Harness star power.

Find well-known people to speak out for your cause. Even if you can't snag a movie star, try to find a local sports figure, a popular local radio personality, a well-known and respected lawyer, doctor, teacher, school principal, or politician, or anyone whose name other people might recognize and pay attention to.

TIP #9: Think of new ways to speak out.

How? One way is to hold a press conference at which your local celebrity will speak. Alert your local paper and radio stations a week in advance by sending out a formal press release. You might be surprised by the amount of press you get. And think often about photo and video ops. Swallow your pride and dress up like an endangered owl or a polluting smokestack. Remember that you want to attract attention (in ways that are constructive for your cause, or course). You want the decision-makers to notice you, *but you're also working to attract the attention of newspaper photographers and broadcast camera people.*

❧ Once we wanted the President to take stronger government action to protect salmon. A group of us dressed up in salmon costumes and paraded through downtown Washington, DC, including in front of the White House. What a photo opportunity for the press. Photographers practically never stopped taking pictures to run in the next day's papers. ❧

❧ Not long ago I participated in a large, well-organized rally at Lafayette Square, across from the White House. This time our opponents were the big oil companies, who were pressuring the President to approve a proposed pipeline through some very important forest and river habitat where a number of critically endangered species lived. Pipeline construction, let alone any future accidents with spills, would guarantee this fragile habitat's destruction and devastate the endangered plants and animals there.

We wanted the President to say no, of course, but we didn't have the money to run ads on TV to get our message across like Big Oil.

What we did was noteworthy and even more effective. Step by step, using the principles and tips described in this book, we managed to get thousands of young people to come out for a rally in Lafayette Square. This youthful horde marched through the square and around the White House, then all joined hands, encircling the building and its grounds.

The sight of so many people hand-in-hand was stunning. The President was astonished—there were actually

more than 12,000 people in the big circle. They just kept coming, and we ended up with a giant ring six rows deep. Everyone commented afterward that this event was a factor in the President's final decision to say no, for now, to the oil companies' plan. ☙

TIP #10: "Adopt" an animal or plant that lives in or near your place.

This is an effective tactic because most people love wildlife and don't like to see it harmed. Some people in West Virginia who are trying to save a certain canyon from development have taken "Annie the Flying Squirrel" as their mascot, named after one of the cutest and most endangered animals that lives there.

This is a good way, incidentally, to engage the interest of schoolchildren. They can't vote, but they can put pressure on their parents! Did you know that data tracked over the past forty years have shown that children who browbeat their parents have been a major factor in campaigns both to stop cigarette smoking and to recycle household materials? Go, kids!

❧ Whenever the following pitch appeared on flyers and in print, it was accompanied by a picture of the club's cute mascot. ☙

URGENT MESSAGE TO ALL
WYOMING NATURE LOVERS!

The proposed new extension of the Shirley Basin Parkway cuts precisely through the forested area where a large population of animals comes to drink every night—including our own Black-Footed Ferret, the critically-endangered mascot of the Shirley Basin Young Naturalists' Club!

If the highway is built, these intelligent, playful, and near-extinct ferrets, along with dozens of other animal species, will be slaughtered by cars and trucks every single night when they cross the Parkway to get to the river.

The Shirley Basin Parkway can easily be rerouted—or the state can put a bridge there, and save countless animal lives! Please join the children of Shirley Basin in saving their beloved black-footed ferret from extinction!

Bonnie the Black-Footed Ferret and her friends in the Shirley Basin Young Naturalists' Club say THANK YOU, THANK YOU, THANK YOU!

TIP #11: Publicize places that have already been ruined.

Photos and maps of places already lost or destroyed can be powerful—the photo below, for instance, is of a formerly wild and wooded hillside in West Virginia destroyed by the mining industry.

If your group is trying to protect a natural area or proposed park, for example, and some threatened places within or near it have already been lost, do something about them. Make sure they're remembered. Sometimes this tactic is known as "the Roll Call of the Dead," and it can be very effective. Almost like part of a mock funeral service, it reminds people that what they once loved but maybe took for

granted is no longer there. We did this effectively during the campaign to save the last redwood forests in California. We proposed a new national park, and every time the timber industry cut down another beautiful grove, we publicized—and mourned—it.

TIP #12: Prepare presentation materials about your issue, and go out to speak to other groups.

The person who does it doesn't have to be you. Find the member of your group who's likely to be best for this job, and have him or her do it, using a Powerpoint presentation or video. One person can go as speaker or two can go together. Community groups such as Rotary Clubs, Jaycees, and others have regular meetings, usually monthly lunches at a local restaurant. They tend to welcome outside speakers to make a presentation every month. Find out who lines up speakers for a given group and call him/her. Don't ask for a speaking invitation; ask for a chance to meet with just him or her for a few minutes to discuss, briefly, how your organization would love to give a talk to his/her group. Take a list to the luncheon itself when the time comes, and ask anyone who'd like to help out to sign it. Then be sure to contact them soon. Welcome them, and invite them to your own meetings.

For presentations like these, get in the habit of making short—very short—videos. With the wide availability of digital video equipment (and people who are good at using it), it shouldn't be difficult to produce an attractive three-minute "documentary" about the place you're trying to save, the waterway you want to clean up, etc. Put the video on YouTube and Facebook.

Videos are powerful. Read the following paragraph. Then read it again, slowly, but with every sentence imagine that you're also seeing images—vivid, evocative frames in a thirty-second informational video. What a power video presentations have!

> **The oil companies want to drill under the ice of the Arctic Ocean. Data show that there will inevitably be spills, which are almost impossible to clean up in that cold climate. Even one spill will permanently destroy a vast habitat for endangered polar bears, walruses, and seals. There are thousands of other places to drill for oil, but this highly vulnerable one *just happens to be the most convenient and inexpensive site for the oil companies to use.* There are no other places for the vanishing polar bear to live. This is the animal's last home. And extinction is forever.**

The oil companies want to drill under the ice of the Arctic Ocean. Data show that there will inevitably be spills, which are almost impossible to clean up in that cold climate. Even one spill will permanently destroy a vast habitat for endangered polar bears, walruses, and seals.

There are thousands of other places to drill for oil, but this highly vulnerable one *just happens to be the most convenient and inexpensive site for the oil companies to use.*

There are no other places for the vanishing polar bear to live.
This is the animal's last home.

And extinction is forever.

Chapter Four

THE DOS AND DON'TS OF MEETING WITH BIG FISH

You're going to have to meet with officials. They make the final decisions themselves, or can persuade their superiors to listen to your message. There are specific ways to succeed in these meetings.

Sometimes a meeting will be a success because the official will agree with you. Other times, a meeting will feel like a failure. But often a meeting that doesn't result in an official's support will prove to be a valuable stepping stone toward your eventual success.

First meet officials to find out why they don't agree with you. Then meet them again with a plan to change their minds, or start them on the road to changing their minds.

Preparation:

🐾 DO prepare. Know exactly what you'll say, and know exactly what you want to learn. The decision-maker has taken time out of his day to meet with you, so have your plan together. He should be impressed with you. He must see that you're committed, knowledgeable, and strong.

🐾 DO study the official—your group's volunteer researcher can help with this. Find out all you can about the person you'll meet with. How long has she been in her current job? What did she do before that? Has she said anything about your category of issue lately? Who are her professional/political friends? Where did she get her education? Does she have any hobbies or favorite activities outside her job? Such information can provide you with useful clues as to things to mention and not mention.

If you can see things from their perspective, you have a better shot at persuading them to see things from yours.

The Meeting:

🐾 DO be friendly and polite. Use their official titles (like Senator, Congressman, Mr., Ms., etc.) Say something nice. Niceness goes a long way.

🐾 DO bring along a few people who care. Of course you can go to a meeting by yourself and achieve what you want. But I've found it to be more effective when I have a few good people by my side. Your delegation is proof that a number of people care about the issue at hand, not just one or two. If the official served in the military, invite an ally who is a veteran. If the official is very religious, have a priest or rabbi attend (who is, of course, already a member of your group). You want people who will help you win the official's trust, win the official's respect, and win the official's support. Think about these factors when picking your delegation. Do your research.

🐾 DO be upfront with your message. Tell the official why you asked to see him. Explain your most important points. If you have other people with you, introduce them and let each have a brief (prepared) word. Hand out the fact sheets/photos. Engage him with your group and with your cause.

🐾 DO personalize your message to each official you speak to. Use what you've researched. If her father happens to be a real estate developer, emphasize why the current development isn't a good idea where it is, and suggest it be put somewhere else instead. Don't give the impression that you're simply against new subdivisions anywhere.

🐾 DO rehearse! Gather your delegation and practice before the meeting. Discuss how you'll handle yourselves. Divide your issue up into pieces and ask the most knowledgeable person to speak about each part, so that you'll take turns giving the official good information.

Go around the room and make sure each person knows what he or she is talking about, and how long it will take to go over the points. And one of you should be the designated moderator, who will begin everything and end it, too.

☙ DON'T come across as if you think this is no big deal. And DON'T ever act apologetic for taking up their time.

☙ DO have literature to leave behind. Write and print a "fact sheet" which spells out the details of your cause. Make it short and punchy. Include pictures of developments that have ruined similar habitats. Paint a picture in the official's head. Leave your material behind so that the official will be reminded about your cause after you and your delegation have left the office.

☙ DO appeal to the official's pride of state, city, neighborhood. Find out where the official is from. Know the areas they represent. For example, some people would be interested to know that a rare species of plant lives in the woods of their own backyard. And most would be displeased to learn that this living thing is on the verge of extinction. Make them understand the damage that would happen if the proposed development/logging/mining/damming project went through. Do your research! You might even learn that this person is an animal or plant lover.

☙ DO state your "ask." This usually takes place near the end of the meeting. Ask the official how he feels about the issue. If he seems unsure, offer him more information. But give him a clear call to action.

☙ DON'T assume that officials know much about your issue already. These are busy people, and maybe this is all new to them.

☙ DON'T EVER threaten. *Ever*. Don't hint, "If you don't help us we can get an awful lot of college students to vote against you." People don't respond well to this type of attitude. You can't persuade with negativity. You want to give the official a positive reason to help your cause. You want him to understand why you're passionate, and then feel good, at least politically safe, about joining you.

❧ DON'T take up too much time. People are busy. Whether you've been allotted thirty seconds or thirty minutes, don't go over your time.

❧ DO be sure to make a polite, respectful impression as you leave. Even if the official said that she can't support you. Ask if she'd like to be informed of new developments in your cause. A decision-maker will almost always say yes to this (nobody wants to come off as closed-minded), and it's critically important to keep the door of access and positive communications open. Even if you get a no at first, you may be able to turn it into a yes. I've seen it happen many times.

After the Meeting:

❧ DO follow up. Write a polite thank-you note right away. Don't procrastinate. I'll say it again: do it right away. If your decision-maker said anything positive, be sure to refer to that statement. Thank her for her understanding and support. Ask if you can come back if you get new information. You can always find new information.

If the official is undecided, use the note to ask what makes her hesitant about your proposal. Call her back several times. But not every day. Don't be pushy. But be persistent. Persistence is everything. Get other people to call or write as well. Show her that many people care about this cause.

If the Decision-Maker Still Says No . . .

Then, well, it's time to ratchet your campaign up a notch. Contact all of your friends and supporters. Tell them what the official said.

Ask everyone you know to call, write, express their concerns, ask the official to change his or her mind. Pour the pressure on. Endless pressure, endlessly applied.

Chapter Five

PRINCIPLES OF VOLUNTEER ACTION

Every organizer is preoccupied with issues of volunteerism—especially how to attract more volunteers and how to make best use of them.

Volunteerism has of course always been the lifeblood of the conservation movement. Seeing that masses of residents have rallied to a cause has an electrifying effect on decision-makers, to be sure, and we've seen sheer numbers of ordinary people tip the scales in our favor over and over again. But the number of volunteers is not the

most important factor in winning campaigns, it's how deeply the volunteers you do have want to win.

Sometimes I've heard people in leadership positions lament, "We can't do very much, we need more members." Of course it's always good to get more members (if they're committed); but what we need even more is members who will fight, the real activists, people who'll stand up and speak out, driven by their convictions and their love of the land. That's really what we must have. How many is far less important.

I'd like to focus, in this chapter, on three important "best practices" in working with volunteers.

1. Recognize that volunteers are very highly motivated to do particular kinds of work. Don't expect people who offer themselves to your movement necessarily to conform, especially at first, to your own action priorities (though they must conform, of course, to your mission and agree wholeheartedly with your overall goals).

It's far more important to get that new person involved in any way he or she wants. If new members want to work where your immediate focus lies, well and good. If not, get them engaged on something else worthwhile that they feel, for their own reasons, would be rewarding, and where their own skills and talents will shine. Later on you can channel them into activities that are higher priorities of your own.

If they want to pick up litter or get more sailboats
on the reservoir rather than fighting for a wilderness
area or against a freeway, let them go for it. This is
important, not only because giving a volunteer relative
autonomy (and showing that his efforts are really going
to be appreciated) will cause him to put his heart into
the work (simply because it's so much more satisfying
to work that way); it's also important because everything counts. It's all important because everything raises
consciousness and makes us that much better equipped
to meet the next challenge, to go on to the next stage
of effort. You can never tell when your litter-gatherer
is going to get turned on to something else. Your job

at this stage is to provide guidance and training right away, and keep that member motivated.

🐾 Such efforts can bear unexpected fruit. Some years ago an ex-logger walked into my Sierra Club office in Seattle. He was upset, he said, about how fishing streams in the western part of Puget Sound were getting all clogged with logging debris. Now, the improvement of fisheries wasn't something we were getting much involved in at the time, partly because there were a number of fish and wildlife groups around who would more obviously have this covered. But none of them apparently felt the need for this man's volunteer efforts at the moment (they had their own priorities and action agendas, of course).

I said, "Okay, Jack, you've just become this district's Fisheries Specialist. You're the chairman. We'll get some cards made up identifying you with the power and prestige of the Sierra Club. Go ahead and start writing letters to the State Fisheries Department and to any other officials you want. Just let me see a draft of everything before you send it out, and we'll get together here every few weeks. Go for it!"

Jack worked hard to clean up some river beds. And all the while he was getting angrier and angrier about the accumulation of upstream timber-related debris. He soon went out and organized small groups of loggers and fishermen, who ended up giving a major boost to the Sierra Club's campaign to reform timber practices around Puget Sound.

My point is not only that this committed, enthusiastic resident was welcomed and put to work right away, convincing him that we agreed his cause was an important one and that his efforts would be appreciated and recognized. I also realize, in retrospect, that the people he found and organized fairly quickly into an effective grassroots body—timber men who were also fishermen—might not have listened to, let alone agreed to work with, some outsider from the Sierra Club. Or if they did, it probably would have taken a lot of time-consuming persuasion on our part. 〜

2. Make sure you're using all your volunteers.

This seemingly self-evident principle speaks to the heart of why many organizations lose members who seemed enthusiastic at first.

Managing volunteers is an art. Don't regard them as commodities to be used when the need for x-number of people comes up. Don't thank them for their willingness to help and then wait for days or weeks to call them to action. Don't think "this particular small job is boring and Joe and I can do it ourselves in no time at all, so we won't use up any 'volunteerism capital' asking one of our new members to do it." Wrong move! Even if a newbie is going to take longer to do a task than you could do it yourself, reach out for volunteer help. The old axiom of Use It Or Lose It applies in spades to assistance that people offer spontaneously. Never invent busywork, but do make sure that everyone who offers his time and energy is put to work right away doing something useful.

3. Watch out for volunteer action, though, that might mess up your own agenda! I've said that working with volunteers to maximum benefit is an art, and it is. It's also a balancing act. A short-term, usually local objective, while commendable in itself and consistent with your own group's mission, could have practical and political ramifications down the road that you might want to avoid. How can this be?

A small but vigorous local campaign to save a place we'll call Fletcher's Creek from pollution, for example, is excellent in its intent. How that creek ends up being saved—as a little victory in itself this year, or as part of a massive victory on the regional level to save the whole district's woodlands and river headwaters two years from now—should be figured out.

To continue our hypothetical example, one danger could be having a smaller, special-focus group of volunteers mount a campaign that alerts developers and local government that the protection of other creeks feeding into the Rust River could pop up as an issue in the future. If this handful of volunteers succeeds in stopping development at the headwaters of Fletcher's Creek, the local development community might think, what will happen with the industrial park we plan to build one day at the headwaters of nearby Cobblers' Creek?

We have to remember that for each of our gains there's going to be a backlash. In this case, the evil developers might launch a behind-the-scenes political effort with their pro-industry protectors on the city, county, and state levels to make sure the whole Rust River region, except for Fletcher's Creek, remains open (through statute and quiet land purchase) to exploitation.

And what if, further, a larger regional organization has had a grand but quiet plan in the works to save all the creeks in the Rust River basin from polluting development? They know, though, that they probably need another two years to lay the political groundwork, raise money, and educate the public before they launch their attack officially.

It would be far better, from a strategic point of view, if the smaller-focus handful of volunteers held off until their plan could become coordinated with that of the larger group. In this case the Fletcher's-focused volunteers' work (timed right) would end up being a vital and valuable component in the larger campaign. The result, hopefully, could be that all the river's creeks—including Fletcher's Creek—become permanently protected.

Here's a story from real life about the phenomenon of filing a lawsuit without regard to its political consequences, a phenomenon I call "Sow the wind, reap the whirlwind."

☙ I remember back in 1974 when a very bright young lawyer wanted to file an action and obtain an injunction against the Forest Service, banning the practice of clearcutting in the Monongahela National Forest in West Virginia.

"Look," he said to me, "I've done the legal research under the Forest Organic Act of 1897. It says very plainly that they have to mark every individual tree. We've got 'em!"

I argued with him, not because I like clearcutting or because I didn't agree with him on the legal point. Fact is, he probably could have gotten an injunction. But then what? Would the timber industry and their allies in and out of Congress just go home and say, "Gee whiz, well, okay . . . We'll forget about logging in that region"?

No way! There would be a backlash of huge proportions, and we didn't have the political strength just yet to withstand it, I told him. Give us some time, a couple of years, so we can build up our political strength in Washington. We're fighting a lot of other battles just now.

But he didn't see it that way, and he filed the lawsuit. And he got his injunction.

Then the deluge came.

The backlash washed all over us. The Forest Service immediately shut down all its timber sales across the whole region, not just in West Virginia. The Southeast Region of the Forest Service at the time included not only such conservative pro-industry Senators as Jesse Helms, but also Robert Talmadge, Chairman of the Agriculture Committee, who was a great friend of Big Timber.

So bills were introduced not only to overturn the young lawyer's injunction, but also to create a whole new management protocol for the National Forests, which later became the National Forest Management Act. All the bills, of course, included provisions that weakened that one legal victory, and none of them had language that we liked.

We had a bitter two-year struggle, and not just against the industry. Just about every southern Congressman joined most of the western ones, plus organized labor, plus some smaller groups, in encouraging the already pro-industry Nixon administration to act against us. What finally passed was an overall defeat for us.

How different it could have been if we'd had those extra two quiet years to work and build up our national strength to achieve a big-picture victory.

Sow the wind, reap the whirlwind. It's a practical and political possibility we always have to keep in mind.

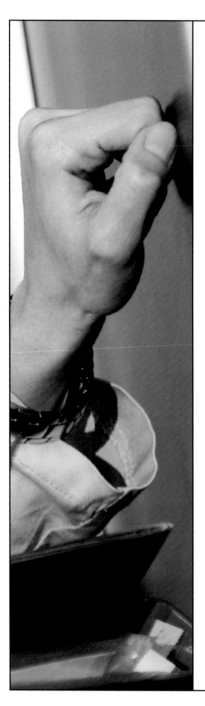

Chapter Six:

LOBBYING LIKE A PRO: THE SIX RULES

Think about it a minute. What is lobbying really? Persuading people to do what you want them to do, even if they don't want to do it at first. If they're decision-makers, it's persuading them to take action to protect the place you're interested in saving. Lobbying is respectful but persuasive negotiation.

You try to find the right message that will appeal to the decision-maker's best instincts, illustrating the specific benefits to be gained were he or she to take your side. Remember, don't focus on terrible consequences.

Be as positive as you can.

Now let's talk about the Six Rules of Successful Lobbying.

Rule One: Prepare your presentation well.

Think it through clearly. It has to be concise, and it has to communicate your message instantly. It has to be memorable. It has to be crisp, sharp, and accurate. And it has to be consistent with what you've already said once, twice, or dozens of times to other people. You don't want your opponents or the media to think that you're flaky because you seem to have a different message every time you speak. Sure, you'll be using different words or ideas, depending on the interests of the person you're lobbying. But it has to echo your vision consistently.

Rule Two: Thirty seconds.

Be ready at all times, and in all situations. You'll never know when you're going run into someone who should hear your message. You must be prepared to make your points in a thirty-second elevator conversation. What if you run into a Council member at City Hall, just by chance? You'd better say something. It might be the only chance you'll get. So give her your message and ask for her support.

Rule Three: The giving and the getting.

Most people think of lobbying as the art of persuading others with your side of the story. But in many cases this isn't the most important part. Sometimes you need to win people's support by showing them what's in it for them.

Whomever you meet with, you must always be aware that they're human beings, too. No matter how important your cause may be, they also have a lot of other pressing matters on their minds. They may even have close personal ties to your opponents that you don't know about, or some background factor that influences them. (In the case of a forest, they might have relatives who own big lumberyards.)

You find out such things by asking:

"Councilman, you've heard our concerns. What's your opinion?"

"Councilman, are you hearing anything from the other side? Any emails or phone calls? Anything else? Have we given you enough information to help you understand why we're here and what we want?"

And so on. This is the all-important "getting" part of any lobbying encounter, in fact of most contacts with someone you're hoping to influence. It's the "ask." "What do you think about this—will you be supporting us? What more information would be useful?"

Rule Four: Listen hard.

Always. Human being to human being. You're not there to tell them your life story (unless they ask). And you aren't there to read them the fifty-page article you just wrote on the subject. If they ask, just hand it to them, with a few brief words describing it.

You're there to find out what they think about your issue. And who, if anyone, is putting pressure on them. It's their vote or their favorable decision you want, and you want to know everything possible about them and how they think when you leave that encounter.

꿍 I remember meeting a U.S. senator from California. We were trying to get his vote on an issue of huge importance both to us and to the very powerful oil industry. That issue was whether or not oil companies would succeed in their campaign to open up a beautiful wildlife refuge, home to numerous endangered species, to destructive drilling.

We all knew the vote was going to be very close, and we explained our concern to the powerful senator. We pointed out that there was literally no other place on earth like this wildlife refuge, so no one should be allowed to destroy it. We said that there are a number of other places to get oil and other forms of energy, etc., but only one refuge like this one.

He was a nice person and listened carefully. Then we asked him, "Well, Senator, what do you think?"

"Well, I agree with your points," he responded, "but I'm afraid I can't vote with you this time. I'm getting too much mail from the other side."

Oh my God, I thought. Too much mail/pressure from the other side? That's doom for us, because mail and public pressure is always our own best tactic, since we don't and never will have all the money and power of a big industry.

We thought it was all over for us. But I screwed up my courage and asked, "Senator, how much mail are you getting?" I reasoned that from a large state like California he could be getting thousands of letters a day. Yikes.

"A lot of mail, a lot," said the powerful decision-maker whose vote we simply had to have.

"A lot?" I said. "About how many, if you don't mind my asking—a thousand a day, two thousand . . .?"

"Oh no, nothing like that."

"Five hundred?"

"No, not that much either, not close. Just a lot."

There was a pause. Then he said, "Well, about fifty letters in all."

Fifty? I thought to myself. And this is in California, and that's what's influencing him? Heck, my own organization has 50,000 members in his state alone. We can do better, much better, than that.

After we left his office I called my organization's headquarters in San Francisco to give them the word: "Senator ____ says he can't vote with us, because he's getting too much mail from the other side. But guess how much he says this is? About fifty letters."

That did it. Our networks went to work and sent out alerts. And for several days thereafter the senator was inundated with thousands of letters and telegrams (this was in the days before the Internet) urging him to vote against the drilling.

He ended up voting with us. ❧

Rule Five: Discover and work with the official's own version of the truth.

Accept one of the most important rules of effective lobbying: the truth to focus on is not what you know it to be; it's what the person you're trying to influence thinks it is.

Your job, as a good lobbyist, is to lead and guide that person, gently and accurately, to that special place which you know is the actual truth. So you need to start out by discovering what the person's version of the facts is: his/her truth.

Often you'll come up against an official's mistaken idea of the truth which has also become a "given" in the press and the public mind. You'll have your work cut out for you re-educating everyone, especially if the opposition has deployed some clever and effective (albeit misleading) messages. To the extent that you can start to alter the public's idea of where the truth lies, you'll find your lobbying of decision-makers much, much easier.

Believe it or not, there was once a time when the dam-building lobby and its allies convinced large sectors of the western population that natural rivers were "a waste"—that rivers "want to work."

~ Google some pictures of Hell's Canyon and you'll see that its spectacular natural beauty is at odds with its intimidating name. The Snake River carves the deep-est gorge in North America as it courses north all the way from its beginnings in Yellowstone National Park to its junction with the mighty Columbia River.

The part we're most concerned about here is the deep-est part: a 120-mile-long river canyon, a thousand feet deeper than the Grand Canyon. Yet it's easily reached by a series of trails wandering through lovely meadows and old-growth forests on either side, or else along the whole river itself. Home to the ancient sturgeon and to equally ancient Indian petroglyphs, sparkling with little white-sand beaches between its great rapids, the Hells Canyon country is a natural wild paradise.

The problem, according to some people, was that all that water flowing through it was going to waste. This was the era, unfortunately, when big dams were on their way to plugging up all the Northwest's great rivers.

"The Snake River: The River That Wants to Work," announced one of the dam builder's brochures. Work? Isn't it doing just fine in its natural state?

But big dams were the order of the day, and their pro-moters held all the political power. There were no envi-ronmental laws at all then, nothing to protect wilderness or wildlife or natural beauty. And sure enough, having dammed up nearly every other part of the 800-mile-long Snake, they applied for a federal permit here too.

That was the situation when I came upon the scene in 1967. True, lots of people who loved this river were very upset. But they had no political power or influ-ence. I feared it was already a moot question anyway, because just a few months before, the only issue on the table was which dam builder was going to get the contract. The different companies were already battling it out in court. Who would be the favored one?

I brooded over the situation and listened sympathe-tically to the pleas of the people who loved this place: please, couldn't we do something, anything, to stop this coming tragedy?

But how? This is a done deal, I sadly thought. Not only are there no laws protecting the environment, out here

in the Pacific Northwest no one even talks about saving any river. That would be considered heresy, just like being crazy enough to oppose logging.

Besides, I thought, who am I? Just a kid lawyer, barely out of law school. Even if we could get into a court by some miracle, what would I do then? We'd be eaten alive by a judge and all those experienced, fat cat dam-building lawyers! (And don't forget that with dams there are secondary economic beneficiaries, as well, beyond the utility and construction companies—developers of waterfront properties, for example.)

But brooding just made me feel worse. So I decided to try something. It was plainly the longest of long-shots, crazy even to think about. But at least it would be something. And I felt strongly in my heart of hearts that all those loving people, not to mention the spectacular river itself, deserved at least some kind of effort. I had to try.

So I prepared and filed a Petition of Intervention—meaning I was asking the judge to admit us to the case, to argue in defense of the wild river and against the dams. I'd never even seen Hell's Canyon, so I made up the actual words of the petition based on what I'd read about. And I mailed it off to Washington, DC.

Hopeless, I knew. But I had to try. I just had to try.

To my great shock, word came back a few weeks later that we'd be admitted to the case (much to the

contempt and disgust, I learned later, of the industry lawyers). "Our first pre-trial meeting of all the
parties will be in the Portland Federal Courthouse on
September 27," they wrote.

That scared me half to death! On the one hand was joy,
utter joy, that we were in, that we actually might have
a very slim chance. On the other hand, I knew the task
before me was monumental. Would I be ready? Would
we lose this thing as quickly as we got in?

I engaged another young lawyer friend so we could
help each other shoulder the burden of a long and
complex trial. At the same time, I knew that a legal
proceeding, even if we did well, would only delay
things. We could only really save the great canyon by
political means—that is, only through advocating the
establishment of some kind of law.

In order to do that, I had to get to know and rally
together all the people we knew who loved the place. I
hit the road.

Soon I was wandering, totally awestruck, through the
depths of the magnificent canyon itself. The place was
breathtaking.

It gave me energy to help organize a fledgling group of
local citizens: the Hell's Canyon Preservation Council.

Now we were getting somewhere. A wave of hope
swept through all of us, inexperienced though we were,

at our mutual commitment as ordinary people to stand up to great powers who had never been defeated before. We're in the game now, we thought, and we're in to the finish.

As soon as we'd organized, the word went out to all river lovers throughout the Northwest: "Come join with us! We're challenging the dam builders! We can save Hell's Canyon!"

And that's how our long campaign to save not only the

Snake River itself but also hundreds of thousands of acres of magnificent forests, meadows, and tributary rivers began. We'd made it to first base now, and even if we had very little money we had passion and energy. We felt that if we stuck with it and never backed down, no matter what, they couldn't deny us in the end.

We stuck with it for eight long years.

These were years of dramatic ups and downs, bitter sometimes, joyful at other times. A newly elected Republican Senator, Bob Packwood, came along, and became our champion in Congress. Packwood introduced the first bill ever to save, rather than destroy, Hell's Canyon.

But we lost in court.

Yet because of the growing strength and visibility of the Hell's Canyon Preservation Council, the judge in the court case agreed to hold off on implementation of the project for three more years, in case dam-stopping legislation got passed.

The new Hell's Canyon Preservation Council became the heart and soul of the growing movement, now nationwide, to save the canyon. Our people were everywhere, spreading the word throughout the whole Northwest and lobbying with me in Washington.

No longer was it a "given" that rivers "want to work," and that, until they're dammed up and generating hydroelectric power, they're being "wasted." For so many years the energy and construction industries had fed this bogus "truth" to lawmakers and the public. We needed to understand the magnitude of the problem before we were able to fix it by changing people's minds.

And our attitude-changing paid off. On December 31, 1975, President Gerald Ford signed into law a bill creating the 652,000-acre Hell's Canyon National Wilderness and Recreation Area. The whole thing would be protected. And the law specifically prohibits dam building, forever. Ꮼ

Rule Six: Observe the dress code.

It's really important always to dress well because that shows that (a) you're serious, and (b) you respect the decision-makers and the office they now hold. The way

you dress, and the other aspects of your appearance, are silent elements of your message, whether you're conscious of it or not.

As a general rule, this means jackets and ties for males, medium dressy "office" attire for females (dress or skirt and blouse or pant suit). Decent shoes, too, please. Sorry, no flip-flops or sneakers. Give some thought to visible piercings and tattoos. Remember that deploying the smartest strategy—making the right impression on the people you're visiting, tailored to what you know or can guess about their own values and lifestyle comfort zones (however archaic and unattractive to you)—is all that matters. You're not there to display your own personal preferences or style. You're there to save the place you love. Don't let any part of your message distract from that. It's not hypocrisy; it's smart strategy.

Back in the days when many young people liked to dress in torn jeans and dirty sneakers, sometimes with untidy hair and shirts, I regrettably had to tell many of my valuable young colleagues that they couldn't come lobbying with me. These were passionate, idealistic, totally committed young people. I could not have asked for better companions or more enthusiastic advocates of saving our environment. But I had to tell them, "I'm sorry, but we can't have anyone's personal lifestyle choices distract from our basic message."

Since you probably don't know much about the impor-tant people you're going to try to persuade to support you, you can't take any chances that they'll focus on the message of our lifestyles or implied disrespect rather than on the message of our campaign.

☙ Sometimes, though not often, actual wearing apparel can have a positive impact. Even a simple thing like the kind of necktie you wear can make a difference. I discovered this startling fact a few years ago when I was getting ready to appear before a U.S. Senate committee that was taking up a major piece of wilderness legislation. I knew it was a controversial subject and there might be strong arguments against my position, so I wanted to look my businesslike-best.

I carefully put on my best white dress shirt and my only good dark suit and shoes. Then, almost as an afterthought, I saw my old Marine Corps tie (with the standard globe/eagle/anchor motif in gold on scarlet) and pulled it out. Just on a hunch I put that on, too. For good luck, I told myself. I had done my military service in the Marine Corps, and I knew that many conservative senators held the (incorrect) theory that environmentalists are anti-military. I didn't want to give them any reason at all, if I could help it, to tune me out. The truth is that even though I'd been out of the military for many years, I still loved and respected my experiences there. My wearing my old tie was no cynical masquerade.

My wife came in and said, "Why are you wearing that tie? Here, put on this pretty pink one." I said, "Honey, you don't know where I'm going today. It's to a tough hearing with a lot of conservative senators who favor the logging industry. I don't want to tick them off any more than I have to."

I went on down to the stuffy old ornate Senate hearing room next to the Capitol. When my time came to testify, I noticed that an arch-conservative senator—one who usually opposed everything we did—was looking at me kind of funny. Then he scribbled a note on a piece of paper and tossed it across to me at the witness table.

Carefully I picked it up and read it. "Mr. Evans, I would like to talk to you about the wilderness bill. Can you come see me tomorrow at my office?"

What's this? I thought. This senator never lets environmentalists anywhere near his office!

I went over to talk to our long-time opponent the next day. The first thing he said was, "Were you really in the Marine Corps?"

"Yes, sir, I was."

"Well, I'll be goddamned. I thought all you enviros hated the military."

"No, sir!" I said, relieved. And we had a good talk, all because of my Marine Corps tie.

Ever since, whenever the appropriate political occasion has arisen, I've worn my Marine Corps tie. ✒

Chapter Seven

ACHIEVE GREAT THINGS WITH THE SUPER TOOL OF GRASSROOTS ACTION: SOCIAL MEDIA

Social media has become a major part of everyday life. It's also, now, the number-one catalyst of rapid, widespread change in all parts of the world. There's never been a force like it in human history.

It gives individuals and small groups a power that no one, ultimately, can control—not big-money industries, not political parties, not governments.

Remember, though, that for all its power, social media is just a tool. Some people think that if they just email or tweet or text more messages to their allies and to the decision-makers, that's it. Game over.

Big mistake. There's still no substitute for direct human contact—especially with our allies and with decision-makers. It's vitally important that you talk to each other and to those whom you hope to influence, as often as possible, in person and face to face. Social media can, of course, help us toward our goal. Here's how:

1. Educating the public. There are countless causes the public would have supported if they'd only known about them. Social media can deliver the news like no other communications system. And with social media a picture is still worth a thousand words. A caution here, though: be thoughtful and selective about exactly which facts and pictures you want to share. Make certain that images show, as accurately as possible, what your place looks and feels like. And follow-up images of what will probably happen to your place can be very effective, especially if you can find images of a similar locale where the same type of proposed destruction has already taken place. This works well with beautiful forests and endangered rivers, to give a likely "before and after" look. "Think about your goal before you post," says Danielle Brigida, an expert at the National Wildlife Federation.

2. Up-to-the-minute updates. Let's say you've just come out of a meeting where someone you didn't know about mentioned your issue—maybe positively, maybe negatively. Through texting and email you can get your whole group in on it right away, and have your colleagues help you track down more information about that person and what's going on.

3. Getting help. There's nothing as effective as grabbing your group's attention with a special urgent email or text, saying "Help! Come to the hearing tomorrow at such-and-such a place and time. Here's our message..." Bear in mind, though, that your message alert needs to be followed up by a phone call to each person.

4. Making friends. Depending on your issue, you'll probably want to have as many friends and potential allies as you can in your address book and on Facebook and Twitter.

5. Snooping. Google may not be able to tell us everything we want to know about a person's character, human foibles, likes and dislikes . . . but it can give us a good start. It can also lead us to those people's own blogs, and blogs in which they're mentioned. Also good: social media profiles.

6. Raising $$$. Let's say a public event is coming up and you want some of your people to dress as animals that live in the environment you're fighting to protect. (This is an old environmentalist tactic—dressing like a Mama Bear and her cubs. It works.) You'll get a lot of attention, for sure, and maybe some local newspaper or TV publicity for your cause. *Make sure your own pictures/videos get maximum public dissemination on the Internet via social media.*

You may not have enough money to make, buy, or rent the costumes. So go to your list and ask! Sometimes, when the cause and the time are right, raising money like this can have amazing results.

If you're raising money in Cloudland, be sure to put together a few great pictures (or, better yet, a short video) showing what you're trying to do. And ask. Say clearly why it's so important that people send money right now—maybe it's a crisis (the bulldozers are already on the way), or a major hearing is coming up. And name a dollar amount you need them to send. Make it a reasonable amount, set out in your text as on a sliding scale (say $5, $10, $25, $50 etc.). Do you know about the new phenomenon of "crowdfunding"? Two good places to start investigating this type of fund-raising are Kickstarter.com and Indiegogo.com.

⁓ Matthew Inman, cartoonist and creator of the popular Seattle-based website The Oatmeal, found out in August 2012 that Nikola Tesla's historic laboratory was about to be torn down. Tesla was the eccentric trailblazing inventor of AC current, a super-star of modern technology. Tesla was given bad press during his lifetime by his rival Thomas Edison, even though Tesla's contributions were at least as valuable as Edison's own in the development of modern electronics. Tesla died humiliated and broke.

Many people feel that the injustices Tesla suffered are tragic, capped by the idea that his historic but long-neglected laboratory building was on the bulldozers' to-demolish list. Actually a Long Island non-profit group had been attempting unsuccessfully for years to preserve the building and its contents as a museum; there just wasn't the money to save it, though.

Inman launched a publicity blitz on the Web through the popular crowd-funding site Indiegogo, and within about a week raised over a million dollars. Inman's message was impatient and eye-catching: *Let's Build a Goddamned Tesla Museum!* Inman's rage that the historic site was going to be torn down so some developer could make a buck was sincere, as was his frustration that a non-profit had been trying in vain for eighteen years to buy the property for preservation.

In May 2013 success was complete, and the property purchased by the non-profit, thanks to the energetic and intelligent social media e-advocacy of Matthew Inman. Work is underway now to turn the place not only into a museum but into a major interactive science education site. ᑫᐤ

7. Free Publicity. Various types of social media offer tremendous opportunities to publicize your issue and your concerns.

ᑫᐤ One of the bigger stories on Twitter not long ago involved some people's following the progress of a wild wolf as he wandered across Oregon and into California. Scientists had put a collar on this young male so that they knew exactly where he was at any given time.

Our wandering wolf developed a following fairly quickly. Some Twitterers pretended to be the wolf, posting tweets, himself, about what he was seeing and thinking about. Thanks to Twitter, many people got hooked on this wolf's odyssey, and as a result became dedicated to protecting wolves. And not a moment too soon: many ranchers throughout the West were lobbying hard to allow the wholesale slaughter of wolves.

And as I write, I'm sorry to say, wolves find themselves again in critical danger. ᑫᐤ

You can follow this example in support of your own campaign. Focusing on a particular animal or bird, even using him as a Twitter "avatar" as the people channeling the wolf did, can have a great emotional effect. The fact is, most people love animals and don't want to see their lives destroyed.

Focusing on the specific endangered species that would suffer or disappear if oil drilling in the Arctic National Wildlife Refuge in Alaska were allowed to proceed has succeeded time after time.

Social media and other vehicles have helped generate thousands, sometimes millions, of letters and emails demanding protection for the polar bear, musk ox, caribou, walrus, and other inhabitants of this unique and fragile habitat.

8. Everybody loves a good video. Even an amateur videographer, but one who knows how to put together a short video about your issue, can help make your campaign a success. In just a few minutes you can dramatize what's happening, and a lot of people will see it. Hey, it might even go viral.

Let's have some more important Dos and Don'ts of social media:

DON'T get into "Clickitivism": the mistaken belief that it's enough just to send an email alert out and ask everyone to click on the link you provide—a link that sends a message automatically to the decision-maker.

Oh, this can be helpful; if the decision-maker starts getting barraged with a bunch of emails about the issue he'll know that a lot of people out there think that it's reasonably important, and probably worth his paying some attention to.

But unless you can deliver many thousands of emails this way, in a short period of time, don't expect a magical turnaround. The fact is, politicians are used to this kind of pressure nowadays. And most politicians and other decision-makers gauge what we can call the Concern Factor.

They realize how easy it is just to click on a link—or, in the old days, sign somebody's petition—and they know that the senders of these messages are not necessarily deeply concerned about the issue. Unless the decision-makers keep getting emails day after day, from new people, they'll probably feel they don't need to be too concerned, themselves, about the matter.

What has to be done next to rev up the Concern Factor is making sure that the decision-maker gets plenty of personal letters, written in the sender's own words. This is the kind of old-fashioned communication that hardly anyone bothers with these days, so it's all the more effective. Especially powerful are physical letters that touch on some kind of personal or family experience tied to the place you're all trying to save, followed by a plea that the letter's recipient make the right decision— and ending with a polite closing and a real signature. That's the kind of concern that does get attention. The decision-maker knows that whoever wrote this letter cares enough to take some time and trouble to express himself personally and non-electronically.

The same thing applies to "group letters," which are the same words as in a single person's letter, but signed (in

their own handwriting) by a larger number of people or groups who are their allies. This can be very effective, because it not only demonstrates that these people really, really care, but also that your cause has a lot of friends and allies—that there's in effect a coalition forming. For this reason it can also be a good idea to type the signers' names and their affiliations under each signature space; for me this is important, because my own handwriting is hard to decipher! Actual, real signatures, though, are a must.

Warning! Don't prepare a standard template letter to decision-makers and then have lots of people send it out. Better to give bullet-lists of points that each letter writer can pick and choose from, but put everything in his or her own words. A decision-maker who receives a lot of letters that are identical will not take the mail blitz nearly as seriously as if the letters seem spontaneous and unique.

Personal phone calls from concerned citizens, of course, can have a tremendous impact. Even if the caller doesn't get through to the senator or congressman or councilmember himself (he probably won't), the official's staff is obliged to make note of, and report, every public comment, especially from that politician's constituents back home.

 We had our hands full in the late '70s. For four years our whole environmental community had been on a national crusade to save Alaska. Calling this opportunity "America's last great first chance," we asked our friends in Congress to introduce legislation to protect over a hundred million acres in Alaska in a great new system of national parks, refuges, and wilderness areas.

A bitter struggle ensued between those who wanted to rescue the best of Alaska's natural heritage and those who supported more oil drilling, mining, and logging. There were fierce debates in both Congress and the national media. But we environmentalists kept on pushing, despite being vastly overspent at every turn by the oil, timber, and mining companies and their supporters. And because we had a lot of public support too (if not money), we were able to persuade the Congresspeople who dominated the House Interior Committee to take the next step in the legislative process: a "mark-up session." A mark-up session is just what it sounds like. All the legislators who are members of that particular Committee go over the proposed bill page by page, word by word, literally "marking it up" with changes.

This is a terribly important step in the political process. If a bill can survive all the political attacks and tweaking within a Committee, then it has a good chance of full passage when it's reported to the House floor for a vote.

The mark-up session on our bill took about three months—it dealt with one hundred million acres of land and was at least one hundred fifty pages long. Despite the complexities involved, we were reasonably confident we would win the final vote.

At that time, the Committee had forty-three members divided up between the two parties. Protecting anything in Alaska was very controversial, and because the oil, timber, and mining companies were against it, so was most of the Republican party.

Our enormous bill involved saving a lot of specific places, and practically every day the Committee members voted on these different localities—to save or not to save them. We environmental advocates were sitting on the edges of our chairs as each place was voted on, because each victory was coming with only a one- or two-vote margin, and sometimes the votes were tied.

Luckily we were winning most of the votes, though, and one beautiful place after another got put into

the final bill for preservation. But one day we noticed something alarming. A liberal Democratic Congressman from New Jersey was starting to vote against us. And a key vote on a very wonderful place known as Misty Fiords was about to come up. It was a precious, "must-have" place for us.

What is this Misty Fiords and why is it so special? Well, imagine Yosemite National Park in California, famous for its magnificent canyons, waterfalls, and forests . . . and now imagine a place four times the size of Yosemite, but on the ocean. Rainforest, deep valleys, huge glaciered mountains, lakes, stunningly beautiful —that's Misty Fiords. And of course mining and logging companies were dying to get in there and start exploiting its natural riches.

Now we had this Congressman whom we'd up till then considered a safe vote turning against us.

Some of us went to talk with him.

"Hi, fellas, what can I do for you?" he asked cheerily.

"Congressman, we noticed that you voted against the environmental side today. What's going on?"

"Look, fellas, I can't be with you all the time. These issues aren't terribly important to my constituents, and you know politics. Sometimes I have to give up something to the other side."

I screwed up my courage and said, "We understand that. But how are you going to vote tomorrow when Misty Fiords comes up?"

"Sorry, fellas. I can't help you this time."

And so that was the word. We stumbled back to my office, shaking our heads. What were we going to do? And there wasn't much time to do anything!

Someone asked, "Where's he from?"

We looked him up in the directory. Camden, New Jersey. Yikes! Definitely not a garden spot, even in the Garden State. But we had to try.

So we got out our membership lists. Wilderness Society, Sierra Club, Audubon . . . and looked for any members with the Camden telephone area code, 609. We found about twenty people. And so we got on the phones. In the end we were actually able to reach only five or six.

"Hi, I'm [name], your [organization] lobbyist representative from DC. Did you know that your Congressman is on the Committee considering the key Alaska vote— and that tomorrow he says he's going to vote against protecting Misty Fiords?"

Yes, it was awkward sometimes, explaining about Alaska and Misty Fiords. But most of these people, being good environmentalists and having read our newsletters, had some idea and sounded like they'd be willing to help. "There's no time for a letter," we said. "You've got to make a personal phone call. He'll probably be in his office between 8:15 and 8:30 tomorrow morning."

It was the best we could do, in fact all we could do, given our limited resources, and the fact that we were down to the desperate last minute. It was our only hope if we were going to save Misty Fiords. We went home to bed, but I know I didn't sleep very much that night.

At 8:30 the next morning our little knot of environmental lobbyists gathered outside the Congressman's door, because that's what environmental lobbyists do. (If we worked for the oil industry we would have swept right in; we would also have taken the Congressman out to an expensive restaurant the night before.)

The door opened. "Hi fellas, how are you this morning?"

"Hi, can we walk with you to the hearing room, Congressman?"

Because, you see, that's what environmental lobbyists do—we get to walk with him for several hundred feet, one of our only lobbying opportunities. We live and move in a world that's very different from that of industry lobbyists, believe me.

The Congressman started talking cheerily about some irrelevant subject, but I wasn't so cheery. In fact my

heart was sinking right down to my toes. We hadn't done it. Goodbye, Misty Fiords.

Just then one of the Congressman's young aides came running down the hall after him. He stopped us all and whispered into his boss's ear.

"Wait for me, I'll be right back," the Congressman told us, and went back to his office.

We waited. About seven or eight minutes later he came out again and was all smiles.

"You guys sure did your homework!" he said. "That was five of my constituents. I'm going to vote with you, for Misty Fiords, this morning!"

And that's how five people in Camden, New Jersey, saved two million acres of a beautiful place in Alaska they'd never seen.

Never let anyone tell you that ordinary people, even just a few of them, can't make a difference in our struggles to protect our beautiful American land. It's the only thing that ever has made a difference, to echo Margaret Mead, for the whole history of our movement. ◆

Chapter Eight
CLIMATE CHANGE

Climate Change (CC), once called Global Warming because of the steady rise of temperatures across the globe—land, air, water, even changing the seasons—has triggered a cascade of harmful effects on nearly everything and every place we know. It affects all living things: both ourselves, and all the plants and animals who share this habitat—known as "Earth"—with us.

These rising temperatures have been the major cause of more severe impacts of familiar (if not always welcome!) events: specifically, much heavier rainfall in many places, thus more floods; more intense, hotter, and longer

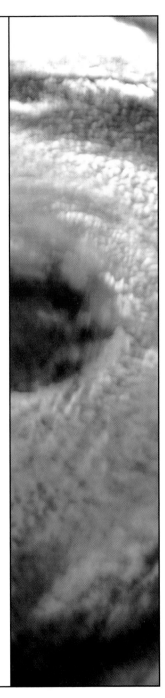

droughts in other places; more storms, all-too-often much more severe and destructive than ever before. Think Hurricane Sandy in 2012, a 1,000-mile long-strike at the U.S. East Coast, with unprecedented damage from Virginia to Maine. Or the more recent "superstorm," Cyclone Phailina, devastating India as I write this chapter.

"We've always had storms, floods and drought," said a scientist friend to me a few months ago. "But now, and increasingly often, we've got something new and different: "Storms on Steroids!" A direct consequence of Climate Change, which itself is a direct consequence of the extra earth-warming mostly caused by human overuse of fossil fuels.

A slight caution: sometimes, where you live, it may not always seem that things are actually getting warmer permanently. Every now and then there is a cold winter, or a cool spring, summer, whatever. These are typical localized temperature fluctuations in a climate process not completely understood yet.

So some people might say: "Hey, what's this about global warming, much less climate change? I was freezing during that unusual cold spell last week!"

The answer is that CC occurs over a long term; while there may be an occasional fluctuation, even a leveling off, other, seemingly irreversible, trends are occurring… and they are not stopping, not even slowing down. Examples: the rapid melting of the sea ice of the Arctic

Ocean and the great glaciers which cover Greenland; and the same for the enormous blankets of permafrost (frozen soil) in the arctic latitudes of Canada, Alaska, and Russia. We don't yet know all the consequences of these drastic changes, but we already know that major species of animals which depend on these specific ecosystems—like polar bears—are fast declining, unable to adapt.

As a zoologist said to me recently about the possible result: "we (humans) will just fry... but they (the plants and animals who cannot adapt quickly enough) will die."

The most important fact to keep in mind is not some local variation; but rather, it is the overwhelming collective body of evidence—and scientists have been carefully monitoring and measuring these trends since the 1980s—now presented to us. Experts are unanimous in their conclusion: that the earth's climate is warming, and that it is happening far more quickly than any previous changes in the past several million years of earth history.

The other near-unanimous conclusion of the experts is this: we humans ourselves, because of our vastly increased use of fossil fuels, in all its forms, are the major cause. That is a sobering fact to contemplate—that we, unknowingly and unintentionally, caused this problem.

But that's good news too, because it means that there are things, many positive things, which we (who will inherit this still-lovely planet) can do about it. It's within our power to make things better, maybe eventually changing or reversing the trends. Most certainly, we can NOW take specific actions to help both ourselves and all the other living things around us, by making these changes… and by adapting when and where we must.

That's what the rest of this chapter is all about: what you can do about it. Answer: a lot!

Before you get started, let's do a quick review of the science, its terminology, and about what others are striving so hard all over the world to do about it.

I. First, some definitions

Greenhouse Gases (GGs): These are the specific gases, mostly carbon-based, which are not able to be absorbed by the atmosphere as they once had been. Just too much overload now. Result: GGs keep being produced, and they spread, like a big, invisible, earth blanket, absorbing the rays of the sun and trapping the heat (and extra moisture from more evaporation) down here instead of reflecting it back into space.

Carbon Pollution: The term applied to a gas (usually carbon dioxide) once thought to be harmless, now understood to contribute most to GW. Too much in the wrong place = pollution.

Carbon Footprint: The amount of carbon it takes to produce a certain product, or carbon-based energy (like gasoline in cars) that the vehicle emits when it

is running. Thus your personal "carbon footprint" is whatever it took to produce that product which you just purchased or how much carbon is spewed into the atmosphere by your car as you drive it.

Carbon Sink: Anything that absorbs more carbon (greenhouse) gases than it releases, such as trees, forests, soils, the atmosphere, and the oceans (perhaps freshwater too). The CC problem of our times is that the atmosphere is so overloaded with greenhouse gases that carbon sinks can no longer do the whole job.

Emission Reduction: This is where we come in. If the normal working of the carbon sinks is no longer enough, and the problem is caused by way too much use/over-use of carbon-based fossil fuels by us… then we know what we have to do, don't we? Reduce those emissions! There are many different and obvious ways to do this; and if we succeed here, we can slow, even reverse, the GW trend. We can also slow or halt the huge pollution and land destruction now caused by the digging and drilling for coal, oil, and natural gas. That's why we have to change, or greatly cut back on, our society's enormous consumption (and waste) of the fossil fuels which dominate today, e.g., oil and natural gas drilling, coal digging and burning, large "gas-hog" air-polluting trucks. This is controversial because those industries that profit from the present situation can and do fight back. Still, as awareness of CC grows, more and more conservation and less waste is being demanded of the polluters. We who care about our Earth should be doing all this anyway. And now, more than ever.

Energy Conservation: This has always been the most favored way to halt wasteful practices and clean up energy-based pollution, and at the least cost. Many communities and states are already well into this field, and are requiring all new buildings, for example, to meet much stricter standards for energy conservation. And now because of a new law (after a forty-year battle between environmentalists and the auto and oil industries) all new cars are required to meet much more stringent fuel consumption standards—meaning, billions of barrels of potentially polluting oil that won't be drilled now, thus not spewed out into the atmosphere to cause lung diseases, or cause more CC.

Forests and Sequestering: It's been widely known for a long time that forests, and especially tropical forests, are a major player in our efforts to control, or slow down, CC. Think about your house plant; it takes in CO_2 and gives out oxygen, right? Now, think of a whole tropical forest, in say, Brazil, taking in and breathing out.

Sequester means to set aside—protect from development—as much of the natural world as we can, especially the incomparably important carbon sinks like trees, forests, and all green plants in general. This can become a huge way to stabilize, then reduce, those emissions. As we have seen above, throughout history, forests have done so, very well, and in balance and harmony with other Earth/climate functions.

That's why saving and protecting as many forests as we can nowadays is even more important than ever before. Now, due to overdevelopment and over-logging, they are overstressed, and just cannot do what they used to. Several recent studies have shown that tropical forests in particular, and older forests in general, have histori-cally absorbed twenty to thirty percent of all the world's CO_2 produced each year.

This is huge. Given the vast global deforestations of the past hundred years, if we can halt and reverse this trend, that alone will help enormously. We simply have to save more forests. And other green spaces too, containing those carbon-absorbing plants.

The great forests of the Amazon in South America are called the "Lungs of the Earth" for good reason. They're being logged at a fierce rate now, mostly to create more cattle pastures. What a waste! Brazilian

environmentalists are opposing this most harmful, climate-changing destruction, and we should help… for our own and the planet's sake.

Oceans, too. The other vital need for more sequestration is to be found in our oceans (and perhaps also some freshwater bodies too, according to new studies). Although we don't completely understand all its workings, it's long been known that our great oceans themselves absorb huge amounts of CO_2. They are still doing so… but they, also, are increasingly overstressed by pollution, too much sediment, and all kinds of trash and human waste. To learn more about this important part of sequestration, and what you can do to help it, check out the website of Oceana, the world's leading ocean protection group: www.oceana.org.

Fracking, specifically Hydraulic Fracturing: This refers to all the activities needed to bring gas or oil, usually located deep underground, up to ground level. Hydraulic fracking refers to a new (and highly earth-damaging) technology which uses huge quantities of fresh water (100,000 gallons or more to operate each well). The water, mixed with chemicals, is injected into the deep well, and forced out into the shale formation—which is known to contain tiny pockets of natural gas or oil. This forcing-under-pressure process causes the fossil fuels to flow into the pipe, and thus be brought to the surface.

It was once thought by many to be a "good" thing for CC, because natural gas produces a lot less CO_2 than

oil; experience, though, has shown otherwise. For
example, where are all those huge amounts of fresh
water provided to each well (sometimes hundreds of
tank truck loads every day) going to come from, and
for how long, especially in arid regions? Two hundred
fifty billion gallons have been used up so far in the
past eight years. Three hundred sixty thousand acres
of once-open space, farmland, and wild places have
been permanently damaged. And homeowners living
near some wells report that their tap water is no longer
drinkable—sometimes even catching on fire from the
methane gas released into the aquifer by the fracking.

So fracking and its impacts (which fortunately have not
occurred at every one of the eighty thousand new wells

drilled since 2005) have become a major part of the CC debate. Those who favor its continuance say it reduces CO_2 production, so it is a "cleaner" fossil fuel process. Those who oppose worry about the damage to our water supply, including the implications of cancer-causing chemicals, as well as land destruction.

Renewables: This is another way to reduce emissions —changing the way we get energy in the first place. Renewables, such as solar and wind power, waves and tidal flows, are usually much "cleaner" with little or no pollution impact. Be advised, though, that each of these methods still has environmental problems which have to be solved or overcome. For example, wind power turbines, if not sited very carefully, can interfere with normal bird migration patterns and kill many birds.

2. Second, we can coordinate with others who are already engaged.

Here are the websites of the some of the leading U.S. organizations who've been working hard on CC and fracking impacts:

www.350.org
Public demonstrations, mass grassroots campaigns worldwide

www.nwf.org
Wildlife habitat adaptation, preventing deforestation worldwide

www.sierraclub.org
Beyond Coal and Beyond Oil public campaigns

www.cleanair-coolplanet.org
Creation and implementation of climate solutions at the
local level

www.foodandwater.org
Lots of good work on fracking impacts on water and
farms

Check these out, read, and learn more. There are
many other good organizations out there with a lot of
experience, some with staff and offices near where you
live. You may want to consider joining their already
ongoing efforts, or you may want to form your own
local organization—and then, by following the tips and
principles in this book, make positive changes for the
better wherever you live.

3. Pinning down exactly what we want to accomplish, and how to go about it.

The best way to start is by following the guidelines,
principles and tactics already outlined in this book.
I've learned that success in every environmental issue,
no matter how big or how small, works best when we
begin as follows:

1. You already know that you care, or you wouldn't be
reading this chapter.

2. After you've looked at the websites above, you may find some that really appeal to you. Join them; and even more, offer your services. All the groups mentioned are very good at enlisting eager volunteers and giving them meaningful assignments.

3. Maybe you would rather form your own group and proceed that way, coordinating with others when and as necessary. Great also! Who else do you know who cares? Friends, family, doesn't matter—as long as they care as much as you do. Talk to them, say you believe we need to organize ourselves, to make things better in our community. Every bit adds up to help us, and the whole earth.

4. Once you've gotten a group, or even one other person, take a look around and see what you want to do about CC. Maybe it's something obvious, like a place where buses, waiting for passengers, keep idling their engines for hours at a time. That wasteful and polluting practice is now illegal in Washington, DC, and some other cities, and there are some specific techniques to raise awareness among the public or decision-makers to change it. Or, say, it might be a dirty coal-burning and polluting electric power plant. Some of the groups mentioned above have done very well in getting such plants shut down, and you can, too.

5. Maybe you aren't sure just yet what could be most effective, but believe there are certainly some things. Ask your building manager or your boss what she or he knows about how well your office building or the school campus is conserving its electricity use. Are the windows insulated to keep cool in and cold out? Does it have an air conditioning system that can be closely regulated so not to overdo it? What about lights and lighting? All are big consumers of fossil-fueled electricity.

6. Let's say you find that your town or city isn't doing much. Then it's time for a Municipal Audit. Clean Air-Cool Planet specializes in community improvement and knows how to do these things. Contact them and see if you can arrange one for your place. The same way with your building. Many towns and cities have adopted tight standards for most efficient electric use, known as LEEDS building standards. Does your town have these? You can find out.

7. Note that all of the above comes under the heading of Knowing Your Facts, an indispensable part of any successful campaign. Once you have that audit, or have gathered the building code exact information, then you and your group have a very strong and credible case to take to the City Council, Mayor, or County Commissioners. Since the main objection is likely to be that it will cost too much, your allies can get you rebuttal information, too.

8. Give yourselves a name. I've read about some groups who call themselves Citizens for a Healthier Climate, a Better Climate, and so on. Your choice. If it turns out to be a good acronym, well and good, but don't use only that. Be sure that your 'official' title explains who you are, as well as sounds good. Remember, your name is a part of your message.

9. The Message: remember how important that is. You and your friends must go over and over what you want to accomplish. Let's say it's getting the City Council to do as they have done in Washington, DC, and New York: give tax breaks and overall encouragement to green roof gardens on flat-roofed buildings all over the city. This is a great idea, because it not only adds more green space to desolate urban areas, but these green roofs also absorb heat.

Did you know that the ordinary black top of a flat-roof building downtown can get as hot as 200 degrees on a summer day? Not only that, but that heat stays there, not getting reflected back… so the whole city gets hotter every night. The green of course absorbs the heat and even can grow food-plants. Roof gardens also absorb moisture from rainfalls instead of letting it all drain off to clog sewers.

If this is what you decide you want to do, your message ought to involve something like "Cool us down," "Let's make a green garden in our city," something descriptive. If, on the other hand, your focus is a dirty coal-burning plant, there are lots of clever and accurate phrases to tell others how you want to stop the dirt and pollution, and so on. The main thing, remember, is that you decide on a clear, catchy, easily understandable (yet accurate) message, and stay with it.

10. Search for allies. Here in this arena, we need bipartisanship as much as possible. That's because too many (in my opinion) leading Republican politicians refuse to admit that there even is such a thing as global warming, much less that humans have caused it—despite all the evidence. This is not the place to discuss possible motives, but I suspect they have something to do with a core belief, plus a dislike of scientific facts that conflict… and it probably doesn't hurt that major donors to some political careers come from the oil, gas, and other polluting industries. Those donations definitely do not go to persons who believe in, and care about CC! I'm certain that many Republicans don't follow their political leaders in such beliefs, I know a lot of them do care and want to help. You should search out these people; they can be great allies, and give your group valuable enhanced credibility.

11. You may want to take matters into your own hands and do an emission reduction project yourself. The students at Camden Hills Regional High School in Rockport, Maine did this and won three major awards for it. Here's an excerpt from a press release describing what they did:

Since 2004, when a group of students called the Windplanners initiated an effort to understand the energy usage of their school, Camden Hills Regional High School students have made efficiency upgrades, researched renewable options, fundraised, partnered with school, town, and state officials and eventually installed a wind turbine on the Rockport campus.

According to the school, the turbine is the first magnetic drive wind turbine of its size in Maine. It was student purchased and is a school owned and operated machine, perhaps the first in the nation at this scale. The turbine is expected to produce 100,000 kWh for the first year, which is currently about ten percent of the school's electricity usage. Over the next few years, through further efficiency upgrades and conservation measures, the school anticipates producing 20 percent of their electricity from wind.

12. Be creative. Remember, our ability to be nimble and to think out of the box can often grab public attention to (and concern for) our cause in ways that nothing else can match. Maybe you're participating in a large demonstration in front of the White House or State Capitol to persuade the decision-makers to pass legislation creating a carbon tax—one of the most effective ways to give companies the financial incentive to innovate and reduce their carbon footprint, themselves.

Always keep in mind that your mission is not just to make a lot of noise and chant slogans. What you want above all else is to educate: the governor, his staff, the legislators, and the media. Especially the last, because that's the key to educating the people themselves.

So don't forget to wear your smokestack suit. Or maybe portray a bird or animal endangered by the effects of climate change and global warming. If you're from the Dakotas, for example, that creature might be one of the millions of migrating waterfowl who once used your states' wetlands, which are now being lost due to drought caused by lack of rainfall but also by fracking, which is sucking up much of the water from the birds' vital wetlands habitat.

13. Walk the walk. This means you! Take a look at yourself and your personal uses of energy and its associated carbon pollution. What is your own carbon footprint? Are you doing your best to use less, turn that thermostat down, turn out the lights, drive in gas-saving ways? After all, we're asking industries, towns and cities, and actually the whole public, to conserve, reuse, recycle, ratchet down—for good—their footprints.

We must absolutely be sure that we are doing the same, every day. Be assured that you will be asked, probably often, "Well, what are YOU doing… are you following what you're saying to everyone else? Are you walking the walk here?" Not only are these important things to be doing anyhow, but they're vital to you and your group's credibility, whenever you appear in public advocating these things for others. The quickest way to lose that precious credibility is an article about one of your group members wasting energy, or otherwise not practicing what he or she preaches.

It's not at all difficult to live a more small-energy/earth-friendly lifestyle. In fact it's fun and will make you feel good about yourself. So, do it!

14. Never give up, and never lose hope. Just keep moving forward and keep trying…and draw comfort in knowing that there are growing millions of people out there just like you, also making things change for the better—every day.

It's so important to stay with it, no matter who assures you it can't be done (and there will be people, who are convinced of it, as in every environmental cause I've even been involved in). Especially in these times, when every day we're bombarded with dire predictions about the Earth getting warmer, and told by some that there's no stopping it.

I swear, I have come to believe that there are some well-meaning people who actually enjoy feeling bad about things, and also enjoy saying it out loud, to make other people feel as bad as they do! Not me. When I read some dire prediction about whatever, I definitely do not want to run home and just feel bad. I want to fight! Push back. Gather around a bunch of like-minded comrades, and see what we can do to make a difference.

In other words, if you love this Earth, love living on it and in it, then stand up for it when it needs it, like now! And never forget that there have been many times in the past when rivers caught fire, people died of toxic wastes by the thousands, precious places were destroyed… and people said then, too, "Well, it's all over, hopeless…"

But—not so! We fought back then and that's why we have the strong environmental laws we have now, and why we have those millions of protected areas, too. Things seemed just as bad then, but many of us said no, and just kept on.

Move forward always, always be creative and seeking allies… and never stop.

Remember, endless pressure, endlessly applied. It works.

Chapter Nine

YOU CAN DO IT

The difficult we do immediately; the impossible takes a bit longer.
U.S. Marine Corps

You don't have to be a Marine to do difficult things. First responders like firefighters and police officers do it all the time, don't they?

Consider those maps with green areas and boundaries around them. Now reflect that each and every one of those places is only there because someone like you loved it and cared enough about it to work for it, making sure it was put on the Protected Map forever.

Please don't forget that there are always commercial forces that sooner or later will be tempted to take over undeveloped, natural spaces and turn them into some kind of money-making projects, forever lost to the creatures who've depended on them for habitat and the humans who've loved them for their unspoiled nature and their trees' life-saving ability to soak up carbon dioxide.

And please don't ever forget that even one person can make an amazing difference.

Sometimes disheartened folks will ask me, "Is that really still true? Look at the huge amounts of money being spent by wealthy corporations and others to get their way, often by influencing our elections. Doesn't that just prove that you can't really protect anything anymore unless you have the special kind of political power that money buys?"

I say no no no. Yes, there's an obscene amount of money being thrown around these days. But here's the truth, and a key to our successes: money is only one kind of power. When it comes to making our Earth a better place to live, there's a greater power at work. I call it People Power, and it may be the greatest power of all.

What is People Power?

It's the power of you, an individual human being. You, who have passion and courage, and—above all—love. Love, which is something the other side hardly ever has where our issues are concerned. We who want to protect the planet don't do it for the money. We sacrifice, we do whatever it takes, for however long it takes. Because we care, which means we possess another priceless advantage, passion. Passion brings spirit and energy to our caring, in a special way that just cannot be matched by money, no matter how much.

I had cause to reflect on this lesson about love a number of years ago:

☙ It was a typical kind of public hearing out there in a small town in the Pacific Northwest; that is, there was a large crowd of excited, intense people, young and old. All gathered to tell the decision-makers why they wanted—or did not want—a new Cascades National Park, which was proposed to be created nearby.

I say "typical" because the large audience was split. About sixty percent wanted the park to be established because it was the only way, at the time, to protect the area's splendid ancient forests, its sparkling wild rivers, its beautiful mountains and meadows.

About forty percent, mostly loggers and miners and workers in related industries, were fiercely opposed to the plan—indeed, opposed to anything that would prevent them cutting or digging in that particular place. They were afraid (wrongly, as it turned out) that they would lose their jobs.

So it was a stormy kind of hearing. There was lots of passion, and even anger. But afterwards I walked across the street for a beer with Andy Wright, the Supervisor of the Wenatchee National Forest. He and his employer, the U.S. Forest Service, were political opponents of the park. They wanted the area left open for logging and mining.

But I liked Andy; there was nothing personal in this between him and me. We ordered our beers and talked pleasantly for a while about a number of things—our families, our homes, the state of the world.

But soon I began to notice that Andy seemed preoccupied. Not only that, but he was drinking more beer than I was, and a lot faster! Something was troubling him and I hoped he'd come out with it.

"Evans," he finally said, "I want to ask you something."

"Sure, Andy, what is it?"

"There's something I just don't understand about these hearings. We've had them all over the state now, and it's always the same with your people. You get these wonderful witnesses. They all have great courage, they stand up and speak out strongly. Our people boo and threaten them, but they stand tall no matter what. And you don't even pay them anything. No money at all. Yet they drive hundreds of miles, some of them, just to stand there and take the abuse, and speak out in favor of the park. . . Our side couldn't do that. We'd have to pay people to drive out here and then stand up before a hostile crowd like the one here. How come your people do it over and over again—for nothing?"

"I'll tell you the answer," I said, "but you won't like it and you might not believe it."

"That's okay. Tell me anyhow."

"The difference between our kind of people and those who support you is one little word, four letters: L-O-V-E. Love. That's what our people have. A deep love for the land, which is why they want to protect it. Love is what our people have and yours don't. And it's why we're going to whip your ass."

And because we're young, I could have added, and care hugely about our future, we bring a very special energy to everything we do. That's another kind of power that can't be matched. Just look at what youth groups are able to accomplish all over the world!

Here are two big reasons why you don't have to listen when people tell you your cause is hopeless so you might as well give up. The first is that nearly all causes are considered hopeless by someone when they first start out. The second is that there's always a way to succeed. Sometimes it may take longer, and there'll be ups and downs. But if you stick with it and decide at the outset never to give up, you'll eventually succeed.

Chapter Ten

A FINAL WORD

Remember those green areas on the map. They're the living memorials to those who came before us, and did what they could to pass it on. Now it's your turn.

I have a phrase for those of us who make the decision to commit ourselves to save a place or a wild living thing, plant or animal or fish. Or a whole beautiful land-scape, wild or not. I call people like us Keepers of the Door.

What does that mean? Well, in my

mind, whenever I think about the latest cause or challenge, or remember what others have done, I envision a door. It's an imaginary door, of course. On one side of the doorway is the Present—all the turbulent swirling ups and downs, joys and disappointments, passions—right now. And beyond that Present, but on the same side of the door, is the Past, with all its passions and ups and downs too.

Here in the doorway, right where I'm standing, are the places and creatures—those millions of acres safe, those species still alive, those strong laws we've already passed to protect them.

And on the other side of my door is the Future. I can't really see past it very far; I don't, or can't—none of us can, really—know the Future. I hope things will be better in the Future than they are now, for my children and grandchildren, and for this precious Earth. It's still our only home, its well-being still the only hope for

all the fishes, animals, trees, plants, and humans who depend on the integrity and safety of their environment.

And so I see myself, and others still alive, as the true Keepers of that Door. Because our job is to push all living creatures and their healthy habitats through the Door into the Future. Every acre, every species saved, pushed through that Door, counts. Safe for another day, month, or year...or beyond.

I don't know what will finally happen. I have reason to hope that things will be better, and that societies will become much kinder and gentler with the Earth in the future than they are now. My generation has fought hard and done the best we could to save what could be saved and to restore and protect, insofar as the opposing political forces could be overcome.

Now it's your turn. If your lives turn out anything like mine, I can guarantee the richest of rewards for you in terms of happiness and satisfaction if you continue to stay on as a Keeper of the Door.

We cannot ignore the threats that continue to tear away our forests, our rivers, our unspoiled open spaces. All environmental causes are important, because the more intact natural systems we save and keep, the easier it will be to slow climate change, and keep our world livable for all the species.

It's as simple as that. You must act now.

Now go kick ass. ᔑ

The author, age three (above), contemplates the
environment. He was still at it at twenty-five (below)
as he is now—with undiminished passion
and dedication—fifty years later.

Appendix

**Putting Things in Historical Perspective:
Selections from the Speeches,
Testimony, and Writings of Brock Evans**

1968
HEARINGS: THE MEDIUM IS THE MESSAGE
Or, How a Bunch of Ordinary Folks Foiled the
Designs of an Unhelpful Committee Chair

1972
THE "ENERGY CRISIS"

1987
BLEEDING OREGON

1987
REMARKS AT CONGRESSIONAL HEARING
In Response To Timber Industry Testimony

EXCERPT FROM LETTER on why
environmental activists don't trust
the U.S. Forest Service

2013
OUR STRONGEST, OUR OWN,
OUR SO SPECIAL—AND SO
UNIQUELY AMERICAN—LAW

1968

Hearings : The Medium Is the Message Or, How a Bunch of Ordinary Folks Foiled the Designs of an Unhelpful Committee Chair

We all know by now how important public hearings are to advance our cause, and we know exactly why: because they often are the very best chance we have to be actually face to face with the decision-makers.

And, since many others will be there, not just opponents, but the media and probably uncommitted people, the hearing is a superb vehicle for really explaining to the world out there just who we are; just what exactly it is that we want/are asking for; and above all, to present as effectively as we can our case... that is, our reasons, well-researched, well-documented, and convincingly explained.

But there are times when all that still isn't enough. We need something more—sometimes a bunch of more of that special "something" to really make our points, and to really drive them home, in the most emphatic way possible.

What is that special "something"?

Simply put, it is US—more, lots more, of us! Bodies, more of our supporters—there—present, in the same room with the decision-makers and everyone else. lots of our people; as many as we can find. They don't all have to speak or testify; but they must be present, if this tactic is to work effectively for our cause. This situation comes about when the issue is very controversial and/or there is a lot of visible and vocal opposition to us. That alone can have an impact on any decision-makers there listening and looking out over the crowd.

And it also can happen when we already know that some of the decision-makers, especially the most important ones, are firmly on the other side. Not a good thing, but that happens too. Since that often can mean there is a smaller chance of getting them to change their minds in spite of our having better facts, a better case, we will need to ramp up the pressure.

I call this tactic "The Medium is the Message." All those new faces can demonstrate, better than any words, that we are not just a few people, but that we have lots of support. Which means political support. ("Do you get it now, Mr. and Ms. Decision-maker?")

We faced just such a problem situation in the last months of the North Cascades National Park Campaign. Remember, we had started out there from nothing eleven years before; in those days, just about every newspaper, influential person, politician, and economic interest group was against us. But we persisted, kept going, never quit... so that by the tenth year of our campaign, a new National Park bill had not only been introduced but had passed the Senate handily, for the Senate was a place where we had more friends.

But now came the hardest part, the House. That's because in the House of Representatives, all legislation about Parks and Wilderness Areas was referred to the House Interior Committee for "consideration." And then, as now, House rules are such that the Committee Chairperson has enormous power. He or she alone gets to decide which of all the bills in front of the Committee will even get any hearing at all. And he/she alone has the power to grant or withhold favors to the other Committee Members, to give them incentive to support whatever the Chairman wants.

Worse yet for us, the Chairman then was the worst possible person: Wayne Aspinall. He not only represented constituents from the most conservative part of Colorado, where logging, ranching, and mining were the only industries... he was personally totally opposed to any more Parks and Wilderness areas. Anywhere.

Thus, over many previous years, Mr. Aspinall had made much use of his Chairman's power to prevent, or at least hold up, most legislation which protected any lands from exploitation. For example, he personally had held up passage of the landmark Wilderness Act for eight years, by delay tactic after delay tactic. And he had done the same with the proposed new Redwoods National Park—again delaying and delaying. At the same time the timber industry raced to cut down as many of the old giant trees before the legislative gate was finally shut on them.

In the two examples above, Aspinall was subjected to a lot of pressure from a number other Congresspersons and Senators who wanted to protect the special parts of this American Earth. But even then, he refused to bend until he had extracted yet more concessions from the park lovers. That's why the boundaries of the Redwood National Park today are so much smaller than we had hoped for, and why it is surrounded by giant logging clearcuts right up to Park's edge. It will be generations before all the scars caused by Aspinall's tactics are healed.

I knew that he was personally opposed to our Park legislation; yet, somehow, some way, the bill still had to get a hearing and actually get moved out of his Committee—that year—or there would be no Park.

But how, given his past record and his open opposition? When he announced that the whole Committee was coming to Seattle for hearings on the bill in April, all of us activists both rejoiced—and shuddered. At least we had a chance; but this was no impartial Committee Chairman, just there to judge the best argument, to call balls and strikes like some baseball umpire. This man had made up his mind for logging and mining decades ago, and nothing ever changed him. He was already 100 percent on the opposing team!

But there had to be a way, some way, I thought; just had to be. After all, there are forty other members of the Committee, and maybe, just maybe, if we could convince them, they would force him to take action.

That is when I made my personal resolve: from now on, and for ever after, whenever any such Committee came out to "my" Pacific Northwest for a hearing, we would give them a show! We would show not only that we had a great cause. We would also demonstrate that we—we alone, and not the other side—had by far the most public support. And we would do it with numbers, sheer numbers of us!

Plus of course all the factual evidence. But here, most important of all, the medium—the presence of all those new people—would be the most important part of our message! That might convince enough of the others, who also had votes, and it might even cause him to think he could delay no longer.

The only way to make this happen was to convince our people that these hearings were all-important. They must come!

So, starting in January, I hit the road. Rain or snow or bad roads late at night, it didn't matter. This was way before the age of Internet, the Cloud, instant emails, not even voice mails... the age of slow rotary phones, for Pete's sake!

So the only way to accomplish this huge task effectively turned out to be also the best way anyhow: face to face, personal, up close. Body language—my own body language, everywhere and to whomever I spoke. Tone of voice speaks too! By that means, plus my words, I hoped to convey the same passion and urgency that I felt about the trials and tests to come.

I drove all over the state those three months, meeting in members' and sympathizers' living rooms, from Oroville to Olympia, from Seattle to Spokane, Yakima to Bellingham, and everywhere in between... wherever I could find persons who also cared about having a new National Park. "This hearing is all important; decisive," I said. "It is our best, and probably our last, chance to get something done. Come to Seattle this April, come and be there... Speak now or forever hold your peace! There may not be another chance."

I also promised that if they showed up, we would help them; we have many friends who could provide lodging, and we would provide typewriters (no computers then) and paper, etc., to write out their prepared statements. "Just please come, and be there; and at least sign up to speak, even if later something happens and you can't. The most important thing is to be there... and to stay there, until it is over."

April came, and there was little more to do, except to make telephone calls and get as many reaffirmations as I could. I rented a suite of rooms in the downtown hotel where the hearings were going to be held, and arranged for typewriters and paper there for those who needed it, or a place to rest, or to socialize with other conservationists whom they had never met before.

We had arranged for as big a show as we could put on, with very few resources, certainly not any money! The other side had all the money to do these things; we just had the hearts and minds, and the love, of the people themselves. But would they do it?

That was my feeling of huge anxiety when the Big Day came, as I made my way downtown to the hotel. Heart still in my mouth—would they come? Would they?

I needn't have worried. They came! And they came and they came... easily filling up the hearing room! And by the time the ever-scowling Committee Chairman came in to take his seat on the stage, followed by the other Committee members, the place was packed!

Yet still they kept on coming, lining up as I had asked them to do, at the table where they signed up to testify.

It was very clear that not only the regular members of the Committee were shocked—so also was Mr. Aspinall, the ever-hostile Chair. He had thought, probably hoped, that it would be just another ordinary hearing, with the opposing sides evenly divided between our grassroots volunteers and industry's paid lobbyists. Then he could say, "Well, okay, it's evenly divided out there in the Northwest, we'd better wait for a few more years ..."

Ah, but now he couldn't say that! By the time the signup line ended, eight hundred people—almost all of them our people—had shown up and, even better, signed up to testify too. I was overjoyed. We had blown this thing—and Aspinall's hope for an excuse to delay—right out of the water, I thought happily.

Even better for our cause in the longer term, all these new wonderful people were getting to know each other. Now, at last, they would know that they were not as alone in their love for the North Cascade wilderness as they may have thought when at home. Most of them had never even heard of the others. I was the only one who knew them all, because I had just visited with them these past months! Now they were bonded together, ready for the future! They could carry forward no matter what happened to me.

Since I was one of the first witnesses for our side and thus responsible for laying out our entire case, talking with the media, and handling other responsibilities, I had asked my own personal mentor, Polly Dyer, who had a great personal presence and was one of the best and most self-organized leaders, to act as our "Floor Manager." "Please wear this green armband," I said, "and anyone who has questions about the facilities, what's happening next, where's the hotel room, can someone help me... I will direct them to you."

So now, with Polly as the superb floor-leader, myself as the lead witness for environmentalists, and those eight hundred people newly bonding, Our Show was ready to begin.

But Chairman Aspinall was not happy, to put it mildly. He scowled some more, clearly not liking this at all. His comfort zone was with all those slick industry lobby-ists, and he knew just how to please them. He was later reported in the Seattle papers as growling, "What is this, all these people—some sort of hippies or something?"

And so he growled into the microphone, having to talk to all those "hippies," saying, "We cannot possibly hear every person here who wants to testify. We'll have to pick and choose." I interpreted this as clearly meaning he would choose one industry lobbyist, then one of us, until the "stable" of industry people present was used up; then disband the hearing. Calling it all quits, and sending hundreds of people home, unheard, and letting him claim things were divided. He had the power to do that, I thought unhappily.

Again I held my breath. We would have to protest any such outrage, talk to the media, complain. But the damage still would have been done. Our whole campaign would come to naught, and no Park either.

It was Congressman Udall, a senior Democrat on the Committee who saved the day at that tense moment. He said, "Mr. Chairman, I propose that we split this Committee in two, and one group goes upstairs, to hear half the crowd, and the other stays down here. Then we can hear everybody, as is our democratic duty."

Aspinall concurred, and that is what happened. All the rest of that powerful day, our people from all over the state lined up, one by one, and spoke from their hearts. All day the testimony was taken down by the scribes and put into the official record. The final result was several thousand pages of passionate, from-the-heart testimonies, all of which said: "We want that Park."

All of this infuriated the Chairman, but he could not stop it, much less ignore it. The Show went on and he was forced to absorb its true meaning: that a great new National Park, not to mention the whole idea of protecting beautiful forests and unspoiled wilderness, was very popular and could no longer be denied.

So that was how that hearing ended: a smashing victory of a Show, the likes of which had never been seen out here on a conservation issue before; maybe not since, either. Never again could anyone in Washington, DC, claim that there were no conservationists, no love for their beautiful wilderness, in my state! The campaign had worked, and we had laid the groundwork for even more achievements in the future. And that Park Bill now seemed doable, within reach—yeah!

But the old fox wasn't finished yet. He had another trick up his sleeve. Noting that a number of the witnesses were from the conservative east side of the state, an area generally hostile to parks and wilderness, he made the following startling announcement:

"Okay, we have heard from everybody here. But I've decided that we need to have another hearing on the east side, to hear what other people, the ones not here in Seattle, really want. The next hearing will be in Wenatchee, five days from now"... and the clincher: " "No one who has testified here will be allowed to speak there, only new people."

Those of us who knew what was up realized that this was Aspinall's last gambit. He knew, as did we, that Wenatchee was deep in "enemy territory." The individual people living there were nice enough, but they were mostly beholden to the logging, ranching, and mining industries. And I had already, in my driving trip, persuaded our best supporters in Wenatchee to come to Seattle! But now the Chairman said they couldn't testify again.

My heart sank again, and all the joy from the victory just won simply drained away. Now we faced a new crisis; probably certain defeat across the mountains in Wenatchee, just five days from now! In basketball terms, Aspinall had just seized the ball back and was fast-dribbling it down the court for a score—with just minutes until the game ended!

Why? Because if we were defeated in Wenatchee he then could, back in Congress, just obfuscate the whole thing, pretend the Seattle hearings were unimportant but the Wenatchee hearings were "the true voice of the people and they don't want any Park." And after that political lie (remember, he was the Chairman) go on to claim that things were "still very divided" out there in Washington state, so no further work should be done to consider a Park bill this year.

And that fact of no more action was a big deal, a huge deal, to us. Because that year was an election year, and if we didn't get a Park bill now, we'd have to start all over again, in an entirely different political environment. Eleven years down the drain, and maybe there could never be such an opportunity again.

What to do, what to do now, after this setback? Well,

we all knew: just had to keep trying, whatever it took. Wenatchee, here we come!

Our story has a happy ending, which I'll compress into just a few sentences.

Our key Wenatchee local volunteer leader, Bill Asplund, and I sat down together and discussed what we could do to stave off defeat and the political end to all we had worked so hard to achieve these past few intense months.

There was only one way to stave off certain failure, we agreed: we somehow must find the bodies, the troops, to make a stand.

Their presence would shock Aspinall, and all the media would note it.

But how, how? All our best people had already been recruited and had gone to Seattle to testify. We had told them what we thought then, that this would be it, the hearing that would win or lose it for us.

And we had won it, fair and square—in fact, smashed them, with eight hundred witness for our side. A shocked and hostile Chairman, still unalterably opposed, decreed this new hearing in "enemy territory" so as to tip the scales back into industry's favor.

So Bill (a teacher) and I agreed that we must hit the phones, finding someone, anyone, to speak out! We called all his adult friends. And we got some, but not enough to stand out. So we went down the lists of his favorite and most aware students... one by one. "Can you come, we will support you, have fact materials, sample testimonies, answers to questions... please come if you care, you must speak now or forever hold your peace."

We made our calls all day Friday. The hearing was on Saturday morning. We finally thought, well, maybe we have enough, maybe... if they all show.

They came.

They came and they stayed. The adults were there. But most impressive to the Committee, as well to the media and the audience, were the several dozen high schoolers who stood to speak. They talked about camping there with their families, and about their love for this special land and their passionate desire to protect it.

Several Committee members interrupted them and tried to bully them with unfair questions which none of them could possibly have answered.

Enraged, some of us shouted out the correct answers, until we were gaveled down. But the kids never faltered, and they never backed down.

And so by the end of the hearings we had succeeded, we had stood, we had fought back. We had most convincingly demonstrated that the new Park had a lot, a whole lot, of support, even there in the ostensible heart of enemy territory.

We had won once again, despite the political odds, that early summer day in far-off Washington state.

1972

THE "ENERGY CRISIS"
Address before the Federation of Western Outdoor Clubs Convention, Asilomar, California

Now, on top of all the other shortages we are facing, this winter we have a petroleum shortage. Because this shortage of oil not only directly affects most of our transportation in this country and also much heating of homes and buildings, and also indirectly affects thousands of other enterprises which depend on electrical power generated by utilities which burn oil, it is being called an "energy crisis." Once again the cry of "crisis" and the demand for urgent and quick and drastic solutions is being raised in the nation's capitol.

What are they telling us we should do? We should turn our thermostats down and drive slower and a host of other things. The phrase "Is this trip really necessary?" will be heard again for the first time since World War II. No one can argue with the need to conserve, for these are things we should already have been doing. We have always lived beyond our energy means.

But at the same time the President urges us to do this, and says he is going to do the same, his Press Secretary notes that he was down in Key Biscayne preparing his energy message. Later he flies on down there again. Two helicopters are also being sent down from Washington, DC, to Florida to ferry him from the nearby Air Force Base to the Key. The whole trip will use up at least 13,000 gallons of fuel—enough to heat ten middle-sized homes for the entire year. And the presidents and other executives of top oil companies jet back and forth in their private planes from meeting to meeting warning all of us that the crisis is at hand, and of the sacrifices we all individually must make.

Are we being had? This is what many people are asking, wondering. Why do the sacrifices to be made always seem to fall upon the little guy—and why are the solutions which are proposed always those which hurt the rich least and help the big energy companies most?

This is an important question, and must be kept in mind as we consider the anomaly of the situation now and the final solution proposed for us by our leaders and the energy companies—"self-sufficiency" in energy.

The concept sounds attractive, and it appeals to that old American sense of self-reliance, but what does it really mean? According to the President, it means a massive effort to meet all of our "demands" from whatever resources happen to be within our national boundaries. It means a speed-up in licensing of nuclear plants, and building more of them; it means a massive effort to get coal and oil shale reserves out of the ground in a hurry, and it means a vast increase in off-shore oil drilling on the continental shelf. It means deregulation of the price of natural gas, and it means suspension of the air pollution and other environment laws if they get too much in the way.

If this is the goal of a "self-sufficiency" policy, there is a terrible price to be paid, and it will bankrupt us financially and destroy our lands and our waters. Because while this policy means all of these things, it does not seem to mean any meaningful attention, in any way, to where we have been going over the past quarter of a century. It does not mean any attention to how profligate has been our waste and our consumption of scarce energy resources. The whole aim seems to be to continue our present rate of "growth" without any attention to the obvious necessity of shaping it or changing it, or even—heresy as it may sound—slowing it down. We simply cannot any longer live in the style to which we have become accustomed, a world of cars that get eight miles to the gallon and where everything comes in triple packages. A policy of self-sufficiency based on this kind of "growth" and energy consumption is simply not worth it and it will destroy much of what makes life worthwhile for all of us. There are better ways out of the present situation, and in the long term, much saner ways to have a rational policy of energy use with a healthy life style, without destroying everything else.

The facts are compelling, and they should tell us something. In 1950, our total energy consumption, translated into terms of oil, was 15.4 million barrels a day oil equivalent (BDOE). In 1960, it was 20.5, and in 1970, 31.6. By 1980, a further jump has been projected to about 45 BDOE.

This is growth of the most exponential kind—just like a cancer cell. It is far in excess of any population increase, and far beyond even what we might call "necessary luxuries."

What does a policy that seeks to satisfy this kind of growth mean? It means, ultimately, about a thousand more nuclear plants. Generally they have to be located near cold water for cooling purposes, and in California this probably means their spacing every few miles up and down the coast. It means massive coal mining efforts, including a great increase in the devastating practice of strip mining, which has already ruined beyond repair and forever, hundreds of thousands of acres of farm and range land which could have been growing food. The effort to develop oil shale resources is also going to take water, and thus not only does it mean the further devastation or stripping of much land but also will have to require many more dams and other water works in an area where water is already in terribly short supply. Where is the water finally going to come from? No one really knows.

The great increase in off-shore oil drilling may be safe in some places, but we all know, from the Santa Barbara experience, what else it can mean. Now they are talking about turning over the immensely productive fishing grounds of George's Bank off the New England coast, and the equally productive estuaries and marshes of the Florida Gulf coast to off-shore drilling. This is important, because even more than potential oil spills from leaks, the real danger of off-shore drilling is in all the on-shore development required. The past twenty years of drilling off the Louisiana coast have seen the obliteration of at least 500 square miles of some of the finest estuarine habitat anywhere, for docks, transfer facilities, storage, barge canals, and the like. The destruction continues at the rate of 16 square miles per year.

This is one part of the price of a policy of "self-sufficiency." The other part means the suspension of the environmental laws which stand in the way. Those in power are going to try to suspend the air pollution laws, for which we have fought so hard, to let them burn dirty coal. They are going to try to ease up restrictions on strip mining, and to hell with what happens to the land. They are going to try to dam-up those free flowing rivers for the oil shale, and they are not going to protect those estuaries when they drill for off-shore oil. And, they are going to do all this and raise the price we pay for all of it, too.

All this may be exactly what the oil companies want, and what the government would like to give them. But the irony is there is no real shortage. There is something like 560 billion barrels of oil in proven reserves all around the world right now. It's not that it isn't there; it's that those who have it may not let us have it. This is a difficult situation, and I do not advocate that we shape our foreign policy to please those who do have it. It is simply a situation unprecedented in all history, where a group of small and weak nations who have a resource that they do not need, for their own use, are telling a group of large and powerful nations—who must have it—that they cannot. I do not believe that this situation can continue. We should at least keep this perspective—that there is a lot there—in mind at all times.

We don't have to have this kind of self-sufficiency, a sufficiency that will go a long way toward destroying the food-production resources that we also need to survive. This policy would ruin the health and shorten the lives of millions of our people, and it would destroy much of our land and pollute our waters. And it would further destroy many of the beautiful places that remain as a part of the American Earth.

There is a better way. Dow Chemical Company, for example, is re-designing its processes and has already reduced energy usage in some of its projects by 50 percent. According to the Office of Emergency Preparedness, better conservation practices and processes in industry could reduce energy consumption there by as much as 10 percent, a savings at present consumption of three million barrels per day. DEP also estimates that with proper implementation of better insulation standards, mass-transit, lighting standards, and other means, a reduction in demand by as much as 20 percent, or the equivalent of six million BDOE is possible. We can revise rate structures by allowing everybody a certain basic amount at a low rate, but requiring those who use more than that to pay higher rates, instead of the reverse as it is now. We can remove the subsidies which we now give to the energy industry in the form of oil depletion allowances, foreign tax credits, and other tax write-offs. We can require real rehabilitation of areas already strip mined, and that any further coal be taken from the massive deposits available by deep mining, which does not destroy the land. We can require full compliance with the air pollution laws, and allow no industry to weasel out of it under the guise of the "energy crisis." All these measures will mean that energy will be priced at its true cost, which will thus further stimulate the efforts to find ways to save it and not to waste.

All of these measures should be coupled with a careful, balanced, and judicious policy of allowing development of new and much cleaner energy sources on a case by case basis where the environmental damage is minimal or nonexistent, and where the costs to the consumer are in balance with costs of obtaining energy elsewhere.

If they are done together, instead of in the panic atmosphere that we have right now, we will still have a clean environment, and a beautiful Earth. And we will still have enough energy to pursue a reasonable life style.

Nineteen-fifty wasn't such a bad year, for those of us who remember it. Most of the "necessities" that we value now we also had then. The air was a heck of a lot cleaner, and a lot less land had been destroyed. We can't go back to that time, but we don't need to go forward into a 1980s of increasingly dangerous smog and pollution and an increasingly devastated earth, just to fuel the freeway-triple package-superneon life style. We only need "self-sufficiency" if we want to continue the incredible waste and over-consumption that characterized all of our use of energy for the last twenty-five years. We could choose if we want it, as an alternative, to maintain our life style at about that of, say, 1962 instead. We would not have to sacrifice anyone's present affluence, nor the opportunities for those who do not have it to get it. But what we would do is cut down the incredible waste, and develop where we must in a rational way in the future. And at least then, we would have something left when we are done.

I will try to finish with some sort of look at the future. What is in the wind for us, for the environmental movement, and for the nation?

There are two major issues that I see now. One affects us and our interests directly and vitally: the issue of de facto wilderness. The other is more a feel for the drift of things, and perhaps a warning for the future, in the sense of new assaults being mounted on existing legislation.

On the subject of de facto wilderness, the time of final resolution is at hand. After two generations of awareness of the idea, with many battles and many laws passed, final decisions are being made. Lines are being drawn, sides chosen for, I think, the very last time. This is because of two things. First, the enormous and growing pressure of the wilderness movement. There are more people back in the woods, and they want more area to protect.

Second, it is the result of the Forest Service's attempt to deal with this process, and they have made some attempts, as you know. They called a series of "meetings" all around the Northwest and the country to hear what the people wanted done with the remaining unprotected wilderness. We disagreed strongly with their process and the manner in which they went about it. They held the hearings quickly, with only a few weeks' notice, literally "up and down" with just a month or two for total input. The hearings for the most part were held in pro-industry towns, and they were held in the winter, when snow was on the ground in the areas being discussed.

We have now obtained an injunction against the Forest Service, forbidding all logging and roadbuilding on these lands until we can have more time for study and input. There will be a trial on this in December. If the injunction is dissolved, the wilderness is in terrible trouble.

The timber industry, of course, is alarmed, and has out alerts throughout the Northwest, mostly in timber towns. They had a special meeting last spring and agreed to spend $4-5 million on ads telling us how we don't like wilderness any more. They are mounting a full-scale counter-attack on us, and I have seen it already in small Northwest towns. Special efforts have been made to close mills down and get the loggers to the hearings. There have been fistfights. A Chamber of Commerce in Superior, Montana, appropriated $100 to buy drinks for all the loggers before the hearing, to get them drunk so they would be more likely to disrupt the meeting and intimidate our people.

It is a bitter thing, and the lines certainly are being

drawn all over the rural West. We have not done badly so far. Our organizations are stronger, and local action groups are working everywhere, documenting the areas we need. But this is the last time we shall have a chance. We are weakest in northern California, and there are magnificent places at stake around the Trinities, the Siskiyous, and the coast ranges. We must not lose these places by default.

There is another matter, which is more of a feeling and a sense of things than something tangible. It's too easy to talk of watersheds and crossroads, and I don't like to do it. But there is a pervasive feeling among our people in Washington, DC, that the environmental movement is perhaps at that point. There is a feeling that our opponents have realized that we aren't going to go away, that we cannot be PR'd to death by buying more ads; the simple buying of more ads by industry telling how many dollars they are spending to clean up won't do the job, and they are beginning to realize it. So, they have turned to new tactics. They realize we're serious, and so are they. This is really nothing new, but we are certainly going to be put to the test more than ever. Industry is digging in everywhere, and if they can't buy ads to convince the people, maybe they can influence the politicians.

Some signs of this are new assaults on the National Environmental Policy Act being mounted. They were started this year, and failed, but they are sure to renew again. An "energy crisis" is building, and there are more and more expressions in Congress that we have to "get on with efforts to provide more energy," and to run over the objections of environmentalists who see the harm in nuclear power plants. Industry is fostering this with its own PR campaigns.

I don't know how to read the future. I do feel our movement has a much broader base and is much more pervasive than many others who are also working for justice at the political level. The problems are more visible and obvious in the environmental field, and they are not going to go away.

All we can really promise ourselves is what Winston Churchill said in the Second World War: "more blood, sweat and tears."

This seems too bad in a way. Why do we always have to work so hard, with no end to it? Why do we always have to fight and struggle without ever any relief? I don't know the answer, but I do know this, and there is a great satisfaction in it, too, to tramp along a beach and know that it is safe, and will not be subdivided because of what we did; to walk through an ancient forest, to smell it and touch the great trees and to know it wil be there for our children and grandchildren; to float down a river that is now safe from dams; and to walk in the high places up in the sun, to smell the clean air and know that that, too, is safe forever— because of what we did. These are my rewards, and I hope that they are yours, too.

Finally, I want you to know this one thing. It has been my privilege and my honor to do this work, with you and for you. It has been my privilege to know the places you know, to go to meetings together, to get to know you, and to fight and share our battle together. It has been my honor and privilege; but it is something much more than that, too. It has also been my love and my joy. It has been my love to taste and feel the Northwest rain forest, the awesome peaks and the high passes. to float down the great rivers. It has been my love to know you, and to sense and feel the common bond of love for the Earth that we all share. That's why we're here and that is what keeps us going.

1987

BLEEDING OREGON
Speech by Brock Evans
at ELaw Conference, Oregon

If you love the great forests of the Northwest and the living creatures that depend on them, it's no fun to be in Oregon these days. Under the prodding of the state's Congressional delegation, the Forest Service and Bureau of Land Management are selling off our public forests to lumber companies at the highest rate in twenty years.

One example: the great uncut forests of Devil' s Ridge, whose 10,000 acres make it the largest unprotected tract of giant trees remaining in the whole state—to wander beside their great trunks, listening for the call of the elusive and rare spotted owl, is to travel back into an ancient cathedral belonging to a time and beauty far beyond our own. These irreplaceable forests are all scheduled for logging—twenty-nine separate timber sales, each of which will destroy, fragment, hundreds of acres of the hugest giants in the next three years alone.

It is the same everywhere else. Despite the warnings of agency professionals, northwest Congresspersons ordered the Forest Service to offer for sale 5.1 billion board feet this year—at least 20 percent more than can possibly be sustained over any period of time, even if one doesn't care about owls or rare plants or campsites or clean water or recreation trails.

What is happening in Oregon is very scary now, and the pattern is the same everywhere across the state: the Forest Service or BLM advertises an uncut wild forest for sale; a conservation group appeals it, then loses the appeal; then the group takes the case to court, and loses again. Then the great forests are sold, and the logging company moves in with bulldozers and chainsaws. Protestors line the roads, climb up in the trees, lie down in front of the machines. They are finally dragged away and put in jail. The timber sale is delayed a few days, but then the timber company files an "interference with contract" civil court action against the protestors, obtains a judgment, and bankrupts them.

Or if the conservation group wins the court case and obtains an injunction against the logging, senior members of the Oregon Delegation simply insert a "rider" into the next appropriations bill, nullifying the court's order, so that the logging goes ahead anyway.

This terrible pattern is escalating all over Oregon. The battle for the last of this race of ancient giants, forests we have dreamed about and thought about from the time we were children, is joined. It is not too much to say that in five more years, at the present rates of logging and selling the biggest and best first, there will simply be no old growth forest left. Yes, there'll be trees, patches in between the clearcuts and next to the roads, but of the forest-homes of the owl, the fisher, the marten—and of ourselves—no more.

There is a way to stop it. It's the Congress which actually sets the amounts and votes money to refinance the "allowable cut" levels. Congress can and does raise or lower the amount of timber cut in the Northwest, and everywhere else. If Congress appropriated less money, fewer big trees would be cut. It's as simple—and as hard—as that. So it is in the Congress that we must join the battle, before we lose it all.

1987

REMARKS AT CONGRESSIONAL HEARING IN RESPONSE TO TIMBER INDUSTRY TESTIMONY

Mr. Chairman, before I give my testimony, I feel a great need to react to what some of the timber industry witnesses have been saying. I have been squirming here for three hours listening to their various points. They need very much to be answered.

You have just heard witnesses for the industry say that everything is very bright for them, that they are now cutting and selling timber from the National Forests at record levels. Well, I want you to know that that is pretty bad news for the rest of us—those of us who believe in real multiple use for the National Forests. It's bad for the wildlife, for the recreation, for the fishing, the water quality, and for the native peoples whose religious sites are there too. It's bad for us who believe in the rule of law, who thought that we had a real multiple-use framework for our National Forests.

One witness pointed to a map of areas on a particular National Forest in my state of Washington which were allegedly set aside to protect spotted owl and other wildlife, as if somehow they were off limits to her corporation and couldn't be cut.

I want to tell you: ***the fact is that they are logging these places too, Mr. Chairman.*** They are logging the spotted owl areas; they are logging the areas "set aside" for the pine marten, and the woodpecker. I heard in a phone call from Oregon yesterday that they just logged the big ponderosa pine trees in the Buckhorn Campground in the Hells Canyon area. Two years ago we had a dedication ceremony for the Hells Canyon area right in that same spot, and Senator Packwood and I both spoke there. Now it's gone.

They are logging over the trails—we've documented a seventy percent loss of trails in the Gifford Pinchot and the Umpqua National Forest in the last decade or so. They're logging the vista sites—on the Ochoco Divide in Oregon, and at Sahalie Falls in Oregon. They are logging everywhere—including the places the lady just said were somehow "protected." They are not protected from her industry.

I am a Northwesterner too, and when she said that tourists don't come there, to Washington and Oregon, because it's too rainy, I had to laugh. *Tourism in now one of the top three industries in each state, just about equal to the timber industry in numbers of jobs.* And they don't come to see stumps and clear-cuts either. They come to see what we have there, the big trees and the forests and the mountains.

There has been a lot of talk of community stability here, and we believe in it too. But it should mean more than just sawmill stability—that's all the Forest

Service cares about. Industry doesn't care about community stability much—they've knocked 25,000 workers out of jobs in the state of Oregon since 1981. And the Plum Creek Lumber Company in Idaho and Montana is busy liquidating all of its forests now. What will happen to those communities after their timber is all gone?

Community stability means more than just the mills. There are other people in those rural communities out there: guides, restaurants, the whole tourist industry, and hunters, fishermen, and people who retire to live there in rural America for the amenities of the place. But all the Forest Service thinks about is getting more logs out.

We've heard a lot about the allowable cut level. The fact is that an Allowable Sale Quantity of 11.9 billion board feet is far too high. It's way above the sustained yield capacity of the National Forests. It can't stay that way, unless we decide that all the forests remaining shall be tree farms for the industry, with nothing left over for wildlife or recreation.

There has been a lot of talk about board feet and jobs. But you should know that things are changing and there is no longer the same correlation between the two as there used to be. New, competitive mills are now being established in my part of the world that cut just as many trees as they did before but with 30 to 50 percent fewer jobs. The typical pattern is that they shut down the mill, fire the workers who are getting paid at high rates, retool and modernize, and then hire a lot fewer of them back at much lower wages. That's what's going on.

You've heard a lot of talk about appeals of timber sales; the industry has said, "We've got to stop all the environmentalists from filing appeals." Setting aside the fact that the timber industry has filed a lot of appeals also, the fact that those appeals are there is a measure of the concern and anguish that many of our people feel about what is going on in the National Forests. Appeals are not lightly entered into, Mr. Chairman; they are hard to do and expensive.

The plain fact of the matter is that the forest plans that are now coming out are just simply not accepted by large segments of the public. It is very painful indeed to see places you love logged off, gone, finished, year after year. That is what people object to. I already mentioned the logging off of the campground and the scenic vistas and the parking sites—it is far more than just roadless areas we're talking about here.

One witness said the environmentalists' appeals some-how represent "minority rule" in the National Forests. I say to you, Mr. Chairman, we would love to have a plebiscite of all Americans about how they want their National Forests managed. We know who would win, because the timber industry's own polls say that the people don't want so much logging and road build-ing. They want a lot less, and they're shocked to know what's really going on.

We would like to have some certainty too. We would like to know that the places we love and cherish are still there, year after year. We would like to know that the wildlife we love and care about is still there, and not eliminated because of the excessive logging program.

The National Forests belong to all of us, by law—by laws that you and the Congress have created. But the timber industry seems to think that they only belong to them. That is the tragedy, and that is why we are here today.

Also from 1987:
Excerpt from a letter from Brock Evans to a Forest Service official who had asked why environmental activists disliked and mistrusted that agency so much.

You asked if I had any ideas for a solution or a way to begin to approach one. I said it is difficult to undo the accumulated grievances, pains and sadnesses, the sense of loss and betrayals of thirty years. Certainly, some new pronunciamento from Washington, announcing yet some new slogan or process, won't change a thing. But there are some things which could be attempted. You know of them yourself, and have probably advanced many of them in various ways in your own work. Here's a few thoughts:

1. (Hardest one of all) Change the defensive rhetoric. Stop saying Congress made us do it, or we don't do it that way anymore, or we just haven't gotten our message out well enough about all the good things we have always done.

2. Do not minimize the opposition or mischaracterize those who are alienated. Comments such as "well, [conservationists are] just another interest group," or, "it doesn't reflect what 'real people' actually think," are, I suggest, self-defeating for those who continue to (wishfully perhaps?) hope that this were actually true. The sense of alienation I think is much deeper than that, and the problem will not disappear by dismissing those who are aggrieved.

3. Set up different standards for measurement of performance. Nothing new here; Jim Lyons, Jack Thomas, many others have said they wanted to change the internal reward system. But it doesn't seem to happen. How about publicly announced standards, such as miles of roads put back to bed, acres of eroded hillsides rehabilitated...and how about really changing thought paradigms and giving recognition for the number of roadless acres given protection from logging, the number of trees above a certain diameter, and the amount of forestland returning to a native/mature status that will not be logged again? I can think of lots of specific measures like this. How about rewards, and ultimately promotions, for these achievements?

4. Stop shooting the messenger, and listen to your own scientists. Take their advice, do not demote or transfer them. If PEER is right, that many of the scientists who recommended more protection for the Tongass now have stunted or terminated careers, what does that tell anyone not within industry about whether that agency can be trusted to "do the right thing"? If the argument is that "Senator(s) Stevens, etc., made us do it," what does that say about trust of a once-great agency? That its leaders will destroy the careers of lower level scape-goats in order to keep their own? Gifford Pinchot and others spoke up strongly when they didn't agree with official policies or pressures. Shouldn't the defense of good science start at the top?

5. Water quality. You mentioned it as a good, popular, type of measure. I agree, but it can also be easily abused. This is the same Forest Service, remember, that has continually insisted that logging in Northwest municipal watersheds not only would not harm them, but was even good for them. How can we construct a measure of "water quality" that will not be used, once again, to justify logging, or somehow to "demonstrate" that logging in riparian areas is okay? Maybe it is okay; I don't have any strong feelings one way or the other. I just don't want to see some vague standard misused to promote some other agenda.

6. You expressed surprise that some groups opposed certification of management practices, as is done internationally. I don't know the situation or reasons for any objections, but two thoughts come to mind:

(1) that what we really want here is to have our own environmental laws obeyed first; (2) that so many of the issues over trust have to do with logging decisions in native forest, roadless areas, prime habitats—they are not just issues over "logging better" as perhaps they might be in Malaysia, etc. Certification sounds intuitively like it might be a good idea if the standards of measurement are at least as strong as our own laws; if the inspectors/certifiers are truly insulated from the Forest Service; and if the standards are understood and agreed to in advance.

Sorry for the extreme length of this. I've gone on far longer that originally intended. But it is a big subject, and has a very long history. I commend you and the Institute for trying to come to grips with it, and to find solutions—and especially for trying to include everybody and listen to their ideas.

I'm sending along, just for your interest, copies of two or three examples from my recent email traffic, which come from the "field" where our people work on a daily basis to deal with real Forest Service decisions. Also the article about the Buckeye Branch Timber sale in Georgia. You've probably already read the court decision in Ohio last winter, striking down the FS Plan for the Wayne National Forest as arbitrary and capricious because it was so skewed towards logging against all the evidence; let me know if you want that too. These are just a few examples of what I see and read every day, from "ordinary people" out there. . .

The problem isn't that the Forest Service doesn't listen or have a good decision-making process. As I said to [an official] today, the Forest Service listens very well—and very often. The problem is that the decisions always come out the same way anyhow: to log, log something. And perhaps the greatest problem of all is that this is a time in our national life when this once-great agency needs a leader who will not only go around the country and say the right things, but also do them, even if he does get political heat for it. Not easy, I know, but these are crisis times, and that's what is needed.

Abraham Lincoln said it best: *Fellow countrymen, we cannot escape history ....the dogmas of the quiet past will no longer suffice for the stormy present...as the times are new, so we must think anew...as the occasion is new, so we must rise to the new occasion.*

Perhaps it is that the present leaders are not quite up to the grave task in front of them, even with the best of intentions and motives. If that is so, then the drift and angst and lack of trust will simply continue until one is found. In the meantime, and until such a person appears, your work to try to grapple with the problem is perhaps all the more important. I'll help, in any way I can.

Brock Evans

2013

Our Strongest, Our Own, Our So Special—and So Uniquely American—Law

Essay on the Fortieth Anniversary of the Endangered Species Act

Author's note: My own personal memories of this wonderful law can never be divorced from its context, the year in which it was passed, 1973. That was my first year as the Sierra Club head lobbyist in Washington, and so my memories of that year are quite different perhaps from those of others more directly involved. I hope readers will be interested in the environmental/political context of that desperate year. To me, they give added pride in the ability of our political system to respond—even during hard times—to produce a law so far-reaching and important to every cause that followed.

But for me that year, newly arrived in DC and with huge new responsibilities just thrust upon me, the Endangered Species Act was way down on my list of even thinking about, let alone considering a priority, then. All that came much later—read on!

Three hundred fifty-five to four in the House of Representatives. Ninety-two to zero in the Senate.

That was the vote on the new Endangered Species Act in each House of Congress, when it was brought to their floors in mid-1973 after several months of hearings.

Three hundred fifty-five to four; ninety-two to zero. "Ho hum," I thought. "Totally noncontroversial. As it should be," I also thought.

The publicity and focus of all the scientific and lay-persons' testimonies that whole year had been on calling attention to the fact that a number of animal species which Americans had cherished, but taken for granted—like the brown pelican, peregrine falcon, California condor, alligator, and many others, large and small— were rapidly sliding toward extinction. Along with many different and increasingly rare plant species.

Noncontroversial—of course! This seemed so obvious. So even though I had just moved to Washington from Seattle (leaving behind both a stint in the practice of law and, most recently, six years as the Northwest Representative for the Sierra Club and the Federation of Western Outdoor Clubs), I paid little attention. The larger, more controversial struggles of the times occupied my complete attention.

In retrospect they were glorious years, those heady times (1967 through 1973) when the nation's young seemed to catch, be a part of, the rising tide of what became the American Environmental Movement. The tiny available resources for any conservation group of that distant era to pay almost anyone meant that I suddenly found myself responsible, on my own, for every action and event affecting forests, rivers, urban areas, wilderness, and other lands and waters, from Alaska down through the Canadian provinces of Yukon, Alberta, and British Columbia, and of course all or parts of our own Northwest states. And not just Idaho, Montana, Oregon, and Washington; I was offered Northwest Wyoming and Northern California if I "wanted" them. And want them I did!

So, doing everything I could both to stimulate and to organize new grassroots groups (and lobby, myself) to protect the still-magnificent wild and beautiful places across my assigned "territory," not only totally consumed me during those years; it was also my entire psyche and world-outlook when Club leaders asked me to move to Washington, DC, in early 1973 to take over (and build up) the Club's DC office—until then more of a listening post than a source of much advocacy activity.

When I arrived that January (with a very tired wife, Rachel; a three-year-old toddler, Joshua; plus our second-born, ten-day-old Noah), my major assignment from the Club was to "do whatever you can to stop the routing of that proposed Alaska Pipeline down across those earthquake zones and dangerous mountains to the sea—Big Oil just wants to sell it for export—and do all you can to secure a more enviro-friendly routing along the existing Alcan Highway to the Midwest, which needs and wants that new oil."

Notice that my orders were not to stop the line completely. We would have loved to do so—after all, its first four hundred miles completely breached the vast wilderness of the Alaskan North, that fabled wilderness recounted in the tales of Jack London (with untold and unforeseen consequences later)—but we were pragmatic then too; the politics just weren't there. Big Oil, the National Chamber of Commerce, and Big Labor were just too strong against us fledgling nature-lovers. "Give it all you've got, do whatever you can..."

Those supremely stressful and intense months that followed were a real eye-opener for a young kid from Seattle. I was both witness and actor, a "Dutch boy at the dike," striving to stand in the way of the juggernauts of all these great powers.

Nevertheless, we fought on, myself and a few Club activists and staffers, and reps of a few other groups. We delayed and delayed the project. We raised a national media storm of support, and I drafted and ran my first-ever full-page ad in *The Washington Post* ... and fought on, until July.

The biggest vote was very close. On a motion by Alaska Senator Mike Gravel to override the new National Environmental Policy Act (which would deny our rights to seek court redress) the key vote was a tie, forty-nine to forty-nine. That meant that the soon-to-resign-in-disgrace-for-bribery Vice President Spiro Agnew voted, of course, to break the tie.

And so we lost, but learned a lot about what really happens in Washington, and how to fight back ... and we extracted numerous pro-environmental concessions along the way. "That which does not destroy me makes me strong," said the German philosopher Friedrich

Nietzsche; and that is how we felt. Stronger. Better able to take on all the battles yet to come.

And maybe now, at last, there would be some time to see what we could do to help this Endangered Species Act, then wending its way through Congressional Committees.

Although it didn't seem like it needed much help. Ho hum, such an obviously needed law, to protect our nation's wild animal and plant life. Ho hum; they don't need us.

Right about then, for better or worse, I became completely entangled in what turned out to be a phony, trumped-up "Lumber Price Crisis," engineered by the timber industry, for the purpose of extracting yet more over-logging out of the nation's already overcut National Forests. President Nixon appointed a Special Commission to review the matter, and again there were many hearings and months more of lobbying, as we who knew what was happening to the magnificent ancient virgin forests of the West Coast fought to stem the tide. President Nixon even then (that autumn) issued an Executive Order directing the Forest Service to increase its timber sales by over one billion board feet a year, so as to "help" the timber industry meet this contrived "demand."

So those next intense months revealed yet another example of how Washington can work; and another lesson was learned about how to push back, by using our own movement's unique power—the grassroots chapters and groups of our people, everywhere, who love their land and will stand up for it when the time comes. And that time has certainly come—again, and almost at the same time!

Just weeks later along came another "crisis." This one began with the Arab-Israeli War, October 1973. The Arab attackers, once they realized they were losing, slapped an oil embargo on the West. Gasoline and oil prices here immediately spiked (up to about fifty cents a gallon, if memory serves me right!) and panic roared through the halls of Congress. And in much of the media too. Nothing like this had ever happened before! In that special "Washington Way" the cry went out for scapegoats: somebody, some things, must be to blame!

So thus came upon us, with me still there only eight or nine months, the nation's first (but by no means the last!) "Energy Crisis." And, like all of them, not really due to a lack of any supply ...just a market perception of such, conveniently fed into by the oil and coal industries and their political allies (still shocked by environmentalists' successes in passing that wave of tough new laws in the three previous years). "It's all the fault of these new environmental laws," they proclaimed; and the President of the Sierra Club and I were hauled before many Congressional Committees to defend those "job-killing" new laws. (Sound familiar?)

So, still no time to help, even to read that new ESA. For by December President Nixon had signed it already. His words expressing the totally noncontroversial nature of this yet most powerful law bear repeating, as a reminder, in these party-polarized times:

Nothing is more priceless and more worthy of preservation than the rich array of animal life with which our country has been blessed. It is a many-faceted treasure of value to scholars, scientists, and nature-lovers alike, and it forms a vital part of the heritage we all share as Americans ... Their lives will be richer, and America will be more beautiful in the years ahead, thanks to the measure that I have the pleasure of signing into law today.

And so 1973 passed on. Everywhere environmentalists and their allies pushed back against Big Oil and Big Coal, whose efforts to repeal the new environmental laws, including the ESA, failed that following January, due to a flood of phone calls and mail from outraged Americans. The ESA had withstood its first test.

For myself, busily engaged in building up a new office, traveling everywhere, helping in other campaigns, there had still been no personal reading time for the ESA. We all pitched in during the first serious new attack on it—over the "Snail Darter" lawsuit, which we won—and saved the Act in 1977-78. Time danced on, and since there were so many good people working to implement and defend the new law, I strongly supported it (and them). But still no read.

The wheel of fate turned, and I became a head lobbyist at the National Audubon Society, charged with protecting the vast heritage of our public lands, especially those still-threatened Ancient Forests, and the Arctic National Wildlife Refuge.

So it was not until the early spring of 1997 that I finally sat down in a less-distracting place (an overnight flight to somewhere) and read the Endangered Species Act all the way through for the very first time. This time, I knew, it was seriously important that I do so: I had just been named as the new Executive Director of the Endangered Species Coalition—an organization I had long admired and worked with.

Now I was its "new" E.D.! "I'd better read this thing," I thought to myself, settling into my plane seat. "In my new job, now, I might be called upon to explain it sometime."

Wow.

The enormity of what Congress had done (and of what those dedicated scientists and my environmentalist peers who had worked on it had done) slowly began to dawn on me.

And it was breathtaking.

"My God, no wonder the far-right politicians, developers, and energy industries are so opposed to this Act!" I thought. "This is the strongest environmental law I've ever seen."

What are the three or four main factors that make it so, this wonderful ESA of ours? First, it states very clearly, that if the science shows that a species is sliding toward extinction, it must be protected, by placing it on the Endangered Species List.

Not "pretty please" or "if doing so doesn't interfere with other things you may want to do, like log or build dams ..." That's the way too many otherwise good statutes tend to work. "Pretty please ..."

Well, pretty please doesn't enter into this at all. If the science shows it (and, by the way, that's "best available science," not "absolutely one hundred percent proven science"), then that plant or animal must be protected. Science, not agency discretion, rules!

Second, a plant's or animal's getting onto the Endangered Species List triggers off a series of legal requirements, the most important of which, in my mind, is that the "habitat" of the species in question must be protected. Forty years of court decisions have refined this notion, but essentially it means that the listed species must have protected places to eat, find shelter, and reproduce.

Third, another specific legal requirement is that the government agency responsible for healing the threatened species (usually the Fish and Wildlife Service) must, in conjunction with the land stewardship agency, devise a "Recovery Plan" which passes legal and scientific muster. That's powerful too, because the whole political reasoning behind the ESA is that it is our nation's obligation to do everything we can to help every endangred species "recover" back into biological health. That is, get it off the list!

Finally, and perhaps even most importantly, especially in these politically contentious times, any person can enforce the law. That's powerful, because all too often in these past decades, some agencies have deliberately refused to put a creature in trouble on that list, fearing a political backlash. Well, we who love these critters and their habitats can't worry too much about back-lashes. They happen, and we should try to ameliorate concerns if we can. But what's the option? Just let it go, hoping that an agency steps up to do the right thing ("pretty please"), and meanwhile watch the critter die? No! We can file the petitions too. We can take a recal-citrant agency to court, and we can challenge habitat and recovery plans too.

Over time, at least half the 1,300-plus species on the List got there because ordinary citizens and their repre-sentative organizations made it happen.

I don't think there's really anything quite like this remarkable law—so strong, explicit, and powerfully enforceable—anywhere else in the world. Which certainly explains why it's controversial in some circles: it works! As intended.

But there's something else.

Since 1997, by my count, there have been well over a hundred specific attempts, in Congress and hostile Administrations, either to repeal or seriously to weaken the Endangered Species Act.

But all have failed. Why?

I believe it's because the Endangered Species Act is something more, much more than a wildlife protection statute (good as it is at being that).

It's also a moral law. And it makes a profoundly moral statement about how we Americans really feel about our land.

Think about it for a minute. In 1973, the legislators of a great nation got together and almost unanimously said, "From now on and henceforth, we the American People shall not permit any other living plant or animal which shares the national territory with us to become extinct."

Now if that isn't a most noble testament to our love for the land, I don't know what is.

Index

www.barclaybryanpress.com

PO Box 409
Port Republic
Maryland